New Mexico's Best Ghost Towns

Two falsefronts in Chloride

for Freeman B. Hover

New Mexico's Best
GHOST TOWNS
A Practical Guide by Philip Varney

Foreword by Tony Hillerman

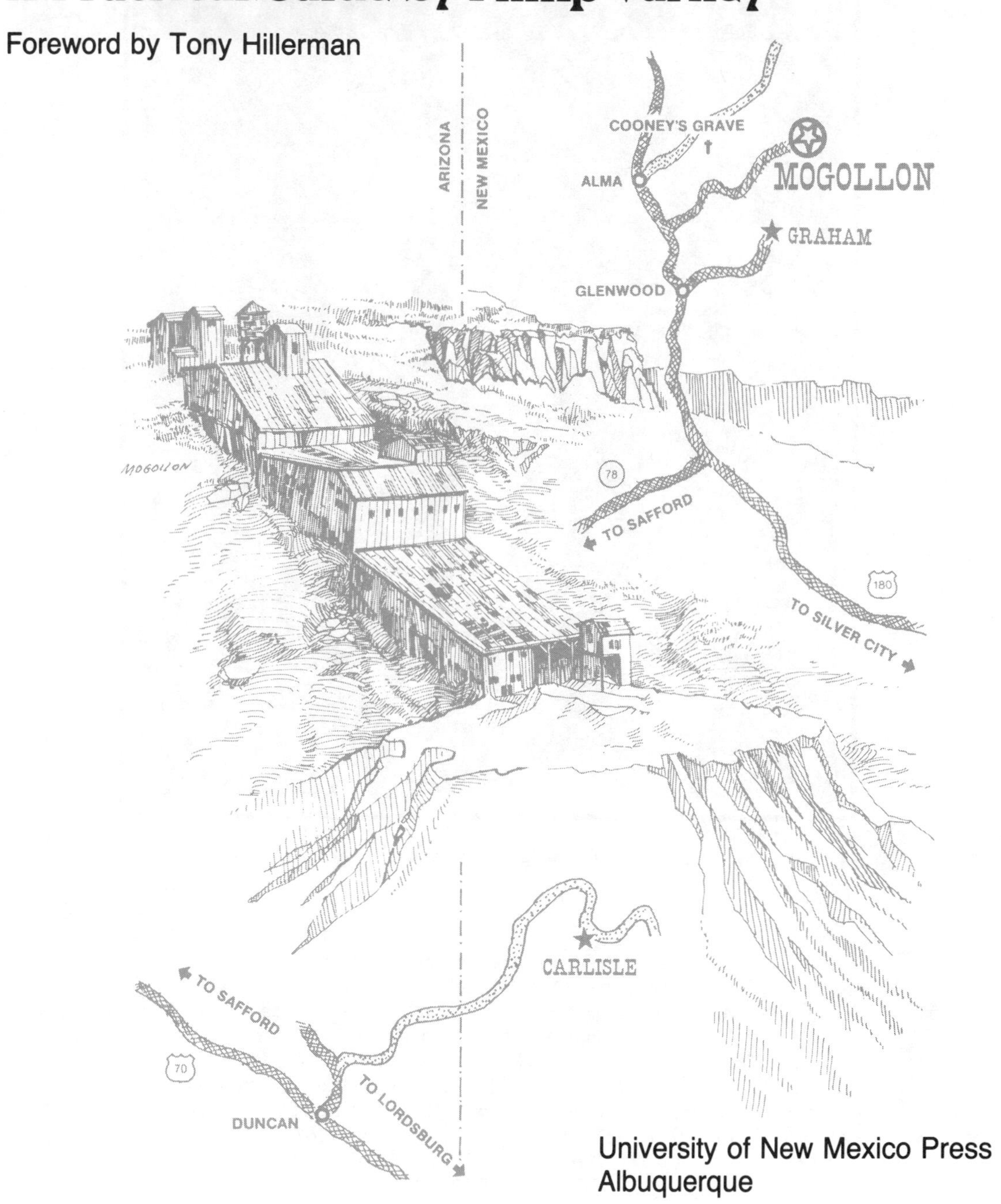

University of New Mexico Press
Albuquerque

Author/Photographer Philip Varney

Library of Congress Cataloging-in-Publication Data
Varney, Philip / New Mexico's best ghost towns.
Reprint. Originally published: Flagstaff, Ariz.: Northland Press, © 1981
Bibliography: p Includes index.
1. Cities and towns, ruined, extinct, etc.—New Mexico—Guide books.
2. Automobiles—Road guides—New Mexico. 3. New Mexico—History, local.
4. New Mexico—Description and travel—1981– —Guide books. I. Title.
F797.V257 1987 917.89'0453 87=25473
ISBN 0-8263-1010-9 (pbk.)
ISBN-13: 978-0-8263-1010-1

1987 paperback edition published by the University of New Mexico Press
by arrangement with the author.

14 13 12 11 10 09 08 9 10 11 12 13 14 15

CONTENTS

FOREWORD

SUGARITE AND SHAKESPEARE. Elizabethtown, Puerto de Luna, White Oaks, Ancho, Baldy Town, Old Hachita, Trementina, La Liendre, and La Cueva. Names that would have delighted Carl Sandburg or Stephen Vincent Benet. Places born for reasons that lost their validity with changing times. Towns that died and left behind their skeletons. Towns that vanished into grass. To me, to many of my friends, to scores of thousands of Americans, these ghost towns offer a sort of touching-place with the past. We stand in their dust and try to project our imagination backward into what they were long ago. Now and then, if the mood and the light and the weather are exactly right, we almost succeed.

It can be a frustrating game, this business of ghost towns, expensive in blown tires and bent oil pans and disappointments. But it's a game worth the playing, and Philip Varney has put a book together that improves the odds. Varney has done two years and ten thousand miles of scouting for us. And since he's one of us—a thoroughgoing ghost town buff—he tells us all those things we really need to know before we start the backward journey.

I am one of the many New Mexicans who own the fine ghost town books done by Pat and Dick Meleski and by Ralph Looney. I've read Michael Jenkinson's excellent work. I doubted that Varney could offer very much that wasn't already available. I was wrong.

Part of the book's value lies in the organization. This volume is a guide book in the best sense of that description. Varney groups our ghost towns geographically so that we could, if we wished, use his maps to visit all of them in something like six months of weekend trips. Everything about the book is practical—from road conditions to whom to talk to if you want to get past the posted signs. But there's much more than that. *New Mexico's Best Ghost Towns* is the product of a man who understands why these old places call us. Read it and find out.

TONY HILLERMAN

ACKNOWLEDGMENTS

I wish to express my appreciation:

To those who showed me the way from their books—Jim and Barbara Sherman, Ralph Looney, Patricia Meleski, Michael Jenkinson, and T. M. Pearce.

To long-time friend Marvin D. "Swede" Johnson and to Luther Wilson, both of the University of New Mexico, for allowing me to utilize UNM Press publications; and to Jim and Barbara Sherman, grateful appreciation for permission to use their excellent book.

To new friends all across New Mexico who opened doors, photo albums, gates, padlocks, and memories: Joseph Kolessar and A. E. Himebaugh of Phelps Dodge (Tyrone); Louise and Shorty Lyon (Mogollon); Bill and Nikki English (Mogollon); Phil and Cindy Fewell (Loma Parda); Dennis Segura and Jenny Freed (Fort Union); Charles Ketcham and Paul Claussen (Baldy Town); Thelma Wynne (Cuchillo); Joe Griffenberg (Las Vegas); Tom Hay (Gardiner); Adolph Baca (San Antonio, San Pedro); Warren Garrison (Steins); Vangie Wellborn and Arizonans John and Roberta Crawford (Hanover and Fierro); and Ofelia Barber, formerly of Elizabethtown.

To special people in New Mexico who have done more for me in terms of information, kindness, and hospitality than a visitor should hope to expect: Rita and Janaloo Hill (Shakespeare); Nick Yaksich of Raton and Kaiser Steel (Koehler, Catskill, Brilliant Canyon); and Corrine Simoni (Cerrillos).

To Chris Ziegler, University of Arizona Library Map Collection, for hours of assistance. Poet and author Peter Wild said there is a special place in heaven for librarians.

To Kaiser Steel Corporation and Phelps Dodge Corporation, for permission to publish photographs taken on their property.

To trip companions, note takers, and navigators Freeman Hover, Charity Everitt, and Allen McGinnis.

To Karen Betzen and Father Regis Tremblay of Salpointe Catholic High School, for darkroom expertise; and to H. P. Madden, for professional developing and proofing.

To G. E. Wolfe, for excellent drawings and maps.

To Tom Sanders and Gloria Feigenbaum of the University of Arizona, for friendship, advice, and encouragement.

To Mort Solot and Roger and Mary Anne Newell, for suggestions on bicycle touring to New Mexico ghost towns.

To Phyllis Kelly, for reading portions of the text and for commenting from a New Mexican's point of view.

To my parents, Tony and Betty Varney, for typing and proofing the text, and to my sister and my niece, Mary and Julie Melson, my unofficial Phoenix sales agents.

And, especially, to Freeman B. Hover, who spent several weeks of two summers and 10,000 miles or so noting, examining, and photographing sites with me; and who, more than any other single person, helped with this project.

TO THE READER

NEW MEXICO'S BEST GHOST TOWNS is the fifth major book to be published on the subject, and a reader might well wonder why another has been written.

I am a ghost town hunter and have traveled tens of thousands of miles in Arizona, Colorado, California, Utah, Nevada, and New Mexico wishing that certain information were more readily available in a book on the seat next to me. To that end, I wrote *Arizona's Best Ghost Towns*, published in 1980. This second volume, like its predecessor, has a clear goal: to respond to the essential questions that ghost town enthusiasts want answered to plan excursions and to assist them in on-site explorations. Those essential questions include the following:

- How much can I reasonably expect to see in a given period of time?
- What are the normal road conditions of the route?
- Do I need more than a road map, and if so, which map or maps should I buy?
- What is actually there at the site, *now,* in the way of buildings, mines, or ruins?
- Is the site open to the public?
- Which are the sites I really *must* see and which ones can I pass up if I don't have time to see them all?

To answer those questions, each chapter provides the reader with:

- a map of the area drawn to emphasize the towns and essential back roads
- individual entries containing current photographs, directions, history, and special points of interest
- a capsule summary of the sites in the chapter, ranking them in order as either "major," "secondary," or "minor" spots
- road conditions, giving the type of vehicle required
- trip suggestions, including approximate time allotments and mileage
- a topographic map information chart, providing names for area maps and the degree to which each is essential for finding and exploring the sites

Every single site in this book was last visited in 1980. Most photographs were taken in 1979 or 1980—and none is older than 1978. Time will, unfortunately, make many of the photographs obsolete, but I have emphasized major buildings and ruins, attractions that one can only hope will endure.

Appendixes at the end of the book give information that the seasoned back roads explorer may not utilize frequently but others may find essential.

- Appendix A will help you learn how to read and use topographic maps effectively.
- Appendix B gives a primer on the most frequently used mining terms.
- Appendix C, a pronunciation guide, can save you the embarrassment of mispronouncing someone's home town.
- Appendix D provides tips for successful photographs.
- Appendix E enumerates basic suggestions for traveling the back roads safely.
- Appendix F outlines possible bicycle touring trips.

Here are some fundamental suggestions for ghost towning:

- Read the section in the book and study the maps before you go.
- Let someone know precisely where you're going.
- Talk to people in the towns: they know the best stories and can make the spots more personally memorable.
- Secure permission to visit spots when necessary. Often a friendly request will allow you to pass a "no trespassing" sign.
- Don't remove anything. ANYTHING. How would you feel if that rusted gate hinge had been removed by the person on the site just before you?
  (*Exception:* Why not remove a film wrapper or soft drink can, even if it's not yours?)
- Take a camera you're familiar with and plenty of film.
- Don't take a metal detector. It is frequently the badge of the vandal. Local residents dislike the device, and for good reasons.
- Carry T. M. Pearce's *New Mexico Place Names* any time you travel in the state. Also have restaurant, lodging, and travel suggestions from *New Mexico Magazine,* which led me to delightful meals at La Posta (Mesilla), Trudy's (Las Vegas), Roberto's (Taos), and at Tinnie's restaurants throughout the state.
- Collect ghost town books. One's weakness is another's strength. Several pamphlets, books, and maps about New Mexico's ghost towns are not particularly valuable, but four fine ones are listed at the beginning of the bibliography (p. 181).

WHAT TO LOOK FOR AT GHOST TOWN SITES

GHOST TOWNS IN NEW MEXICO range from the spectacular and nearly complete to the devastated and virtually vanished. That does not mean, however, that only the major sites are worth visiting; often the remote and deteriorated foundations at the end of a dirt road offer a satisfaction and solitude that larger, more accessible towns lack. And, after some practice, you will see more at a sparse site than a person who doesn't know what to look for.

New Mexico is somewhat unusual, for in this book's collection of over eighty sites, only forty-three are mining towns. By comparison, my book on Arizona ghost towns contains eighty-one entries, seventy-one of which are mining-related. New Mexico has wonderful variety. About a dozen sites in this book lived and died because of the railroads. Over two dozen were doomed because of the urbanization of the West—they were farming and ranching communities whose hard ways of life became unattractive to people lured to the cities. A few were ghost town oddities, a "miscellaneous" category: towns near military forts that died when the fort was abandoned; a lumber town that went under when the timber gave out; a land speculator's dream that went sour; a resort that eventually couldn't break even.

At such sites, evidence of the town's lifestyle is as varied as the cause of its existence. At railroad towns like Hachita and Columbus, you will still see stations and water towers. At others, only roadbeds mark the route of the tracks. Ranching and farming towns like La Liendre, Trementina, and Valverde are often remote and have a desolation that makes them particularly attractive, but buildings there were usually not as durable as more permanent, settled sites. Often only foundations, walls, or cemeteries remain.

Mining towns are different. The least permanent sites are those where only placer deposits were worked (see Appendix B, p. 173, for definitions of "placer" and other mining terms). At placer sites, you will find extensive disturbance of the streambed (see photograph taken near Baldy Town, p. 43).

More promising for ghost town enthusiasts are communities that formed around mines and mills. The mines usually feature adits with waste dumps on hillsides as well as shafts with headframes on more level ground. (See photographs of headframes with the entries of Gamerco (p. 34), Kelly (p. 92), Hanover (p. 122), and Old Hachita (p. 145).

Mills usually stand longer than residential or commercial buildings because they were of heavier construction and more difficult to move. Even if the mills have been dismantled or destroyed, the sites they once occupied are often prominent since the mills were often built into the sides of hills to minimize the amount of foundation work. One of the best mills in the West stands at the Little Fannie Mine at Mogollon (see photographs, pages 160 and 165). An example of a site where just the foundation remains can be found at nearby Graham (see photograph, p. 159).

Heavy-duty buildings like smelters, ovens, powerhouses, and chimneys can stand for generations. Smelter remains are not common in New Mexico, however, probably because of the early presence of the railroad. Ore was frequently transported to places like El Paso, Texas, and Douglas, Arizona, because it was cheaper than building a smelter at a mine site. Coke and charcoal ovens abound in the Raton area, but only Gardiner's are visible from public property. (See photographs of Dawson (p. 48), and Catskill (pp. 51 and 52). For photographs of powerhouse ruins and chimneys, see Dawson (p. 48), Brilliant Canyon (p. 53), and Carlisle (p. 158).

Residential and municipal buildings—schools, churches, and the like—tend to survive longer if they are rock or stone, such as those at Elizabethtown and Puerto de Luna (see photographs, pp. 40 and 64). An adobe structure can endure for centuries *if* it has a roof. When the roof collapses, the building will deteriorate rapidly as rain washes the walls. Compare, for example, the 1894 church at Cabezon (photograph, p. 32) to the roofless adobe ruin at Coyote (photograph, p. 11), erected at least ten years later.

Some of my favorite excursions to ghost towns have been highlighted by stops at their cemeteries. Several things make cemeteries memorable: the varied sizes, materials, and designs of grave markers; the verses on the markers, mostly doggerel but occasionally eloquent—and certainly heartfelt; and, perhaps most importantly, the speculations on the lives of the people buried there—the unanswered puzzles that tombstones often pose.

A ghost town, to me, is any site that has had a markedly decreased population from its peak, a town whose initial reason for settlement (like a mine or a railroad) no longer keeps people in the community. A ghost town, then, can be completely abandoned, like Loma Parda (p. 23) and Valverde (p. 87); it can have a resident or two, like Cabezon (p. 31) and Shakespeare (p. 129); or it can be a town with genuine signs of vitality, like Madrid (p. 1) and Hillsboro (p. 108). Towns like Madrid are definitely ghosts in the wider sense. Schools and churches are vacant or are used as residences. Hotels are boarded. Municipal services are at a minimum.

People living in ghost towns are occasionally defensive, sometimes downright hostile. They may resent being considered a curiosity, and they have watched with fury as visitors have pillaged their home towns. Can we blame them? On the other hand, some of the warmest, most generous people I have ever met live in these towns. It is your responsibility to assuage the doubters with polite assurances and to convince the friendly that you won't betray their affability by disturbing the remnants of the town they live in. But don't ignore the residents, for if you go to an inhabited ghost town and meet only ghosts, you will have neglected the town's greatest treasure.

A WORD OF CAUTION ABOUT DIRECTIONS AND MAPS

EACH ENTRY BEGINS with directions that were accurate when the site was visited in 1980. Of course, changes can occur over the years: a new road could bypass the site; a locked gate could be put across the only access; or, tragically, an entire site could be razed or burned.

The maps accompanying this book are not intended to replace topographic maps when sites are far from main roads. The maps are intended to give a clear picture of the towns' positions relative to main roads, larger towns, and other ghost town sites. The reader will need to use the maps in conjunction with the written directions for each entry and occasionally with one or more topographic maps. At the end of each chapter is a section that tells the reader which topographic maps are essential.

AREAS OF NEW MEXICO COVERED BY THE CHAPTERS

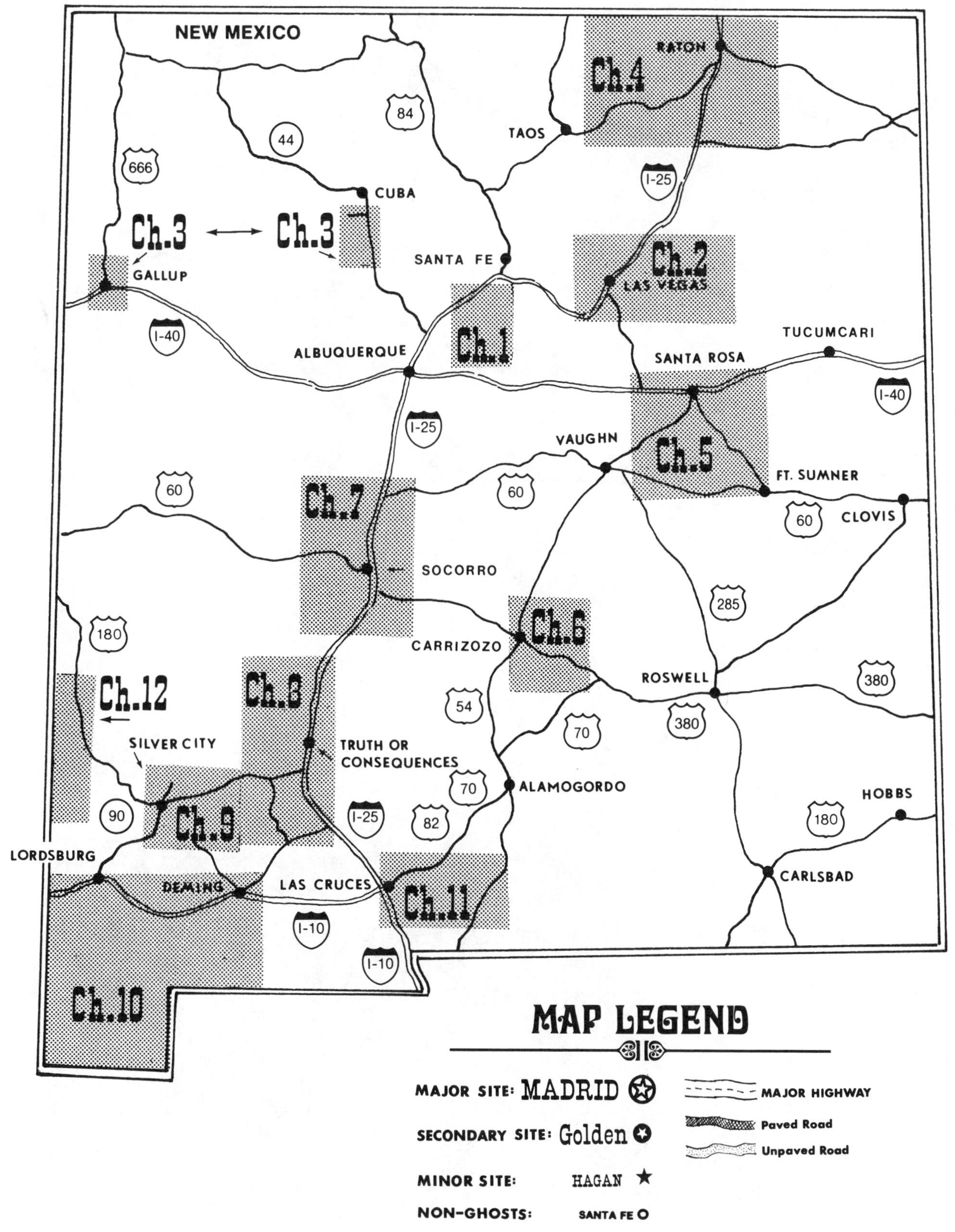

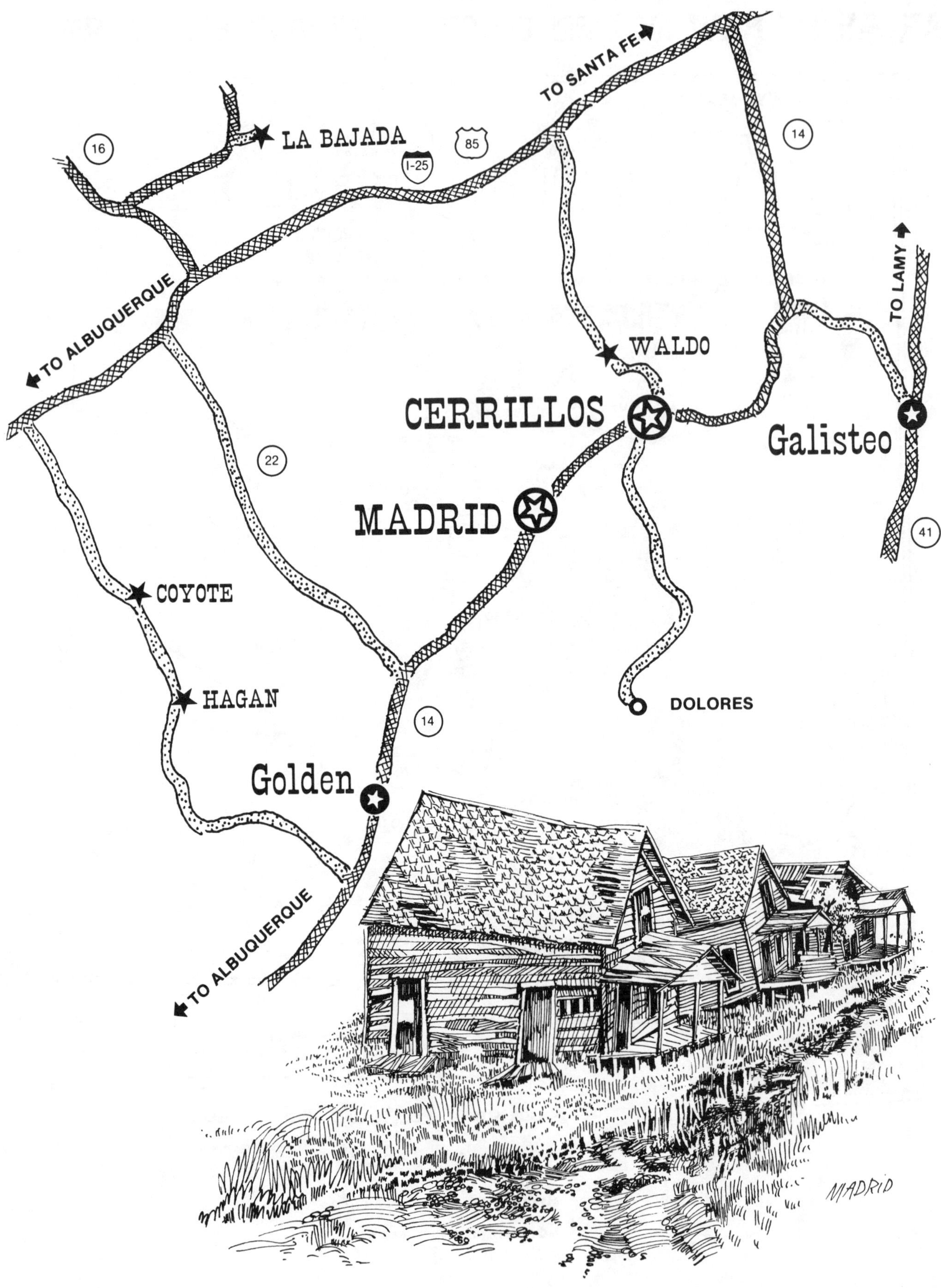
TO SANTA FE
16
LA BAJADA
85
I-25
14
TO LAMY
TO ALBUQUERQUE
WALDO
CERRILLOS
Galisteo
22
MADRID
41
COYOTE
HAGAN
DOLORES
14
Golden
TO ALBUQUERQUE
MADRID

CHAPTER ONE

GOLD AND COAL IN THE ORTIZ MOUNTAINS

A NATURAL STARTING POINT for a book about New Mexico's ghost towns is the Ortiz Mountains, for ghost towns are usually mining towns, and it was here, south of Santa Fe, that the first New Mexican gold rush occurred. In 1829, twenty years before the mad rush to Sutter's Mill on the American River in California, a Mexican herder followed stray sheep into the Ortiz Mountains and found gold-bearing ore. From all over Mexico people scurried to the area, and a community known as El Real de Dolores (also called Dolores Camp) boasted a population of approximately three thousand only a few months later.

Dolores, also known as Old Placers, is private property now, and mining operations have reopened there. Many other sites, however, are open to visitors, including one of the best in the state—Madrid.

MADRID

Madrid is about 27 miles south of Santa Fe on New Mexico 14 and 3 miles south of Cerrillos.

Coal, almost thirty square miles of it, first brought people to the Madrid area as early as 1835. In the 1920s and 1930s, people came each December to view the Christmas City, the town of forty thousand light bulbs and countless displays of nativity and secular scenes. Now it is the ghostly remains of Madrid that draw the people — rows of wooden company houses, the miners' amusement hall, the old Catholic church, and the coal mining museum. But Madrid today seems to be a town divided against itself. One faction advertises rock concerts at the ball park on Albuquerque radio, seeks tourists through brochures about the Turquoise Trail, and touts businesses with addresses on Ghost Town Plaza. The other element resents tourists drawn to the area, displaying a sign proclaiming "This is *not* a ghost town!" and glaring at the people who have dared to come to their community. As a result, a visit to one of New Mexico's very best ghost towns is frustrating because residents seem alternately welcoming and surly. There can be no doubt that some tourists have damaged Madrid, but far more visitors have infinite respect for the haunted beauty of the town and do not deserve the treatment they often receive. The most devastating destruction in recent years was not carried out by tourists but rather by the commercial interests that tore down, in the spring of 1980, the magnificent old breaker building that used to rise like a rickety hulk above the town's other structures. Now it resembles a giant's game of pick-up sticks.

Madrid (local pronunciation accents it on the first syllable) was founded about 1869, but it wasn't until the Santa Fe railroad brought a spur

Garage in Madrid's coal mine museum

to the town in the 1880s that coal mining began on a large scale. Bituminous and anthracite coal were found in adjoining seams in the mines; in one case soft coal was extracted from one side of a tunnel while hard coal was taken from the other. One shaft went to a depth of almost three thousand feet.

The Albuquerque and Cerrillos Coal Company provided for the four thousand people who once lived in Madrid by offering housing at two dollars per month and operating a variety of company stores, including an automobile agency. The company also brought in 120,000 to 160,000 gallons of water per day from Waldo in tank cars, offered complete medical care for three dollars per month, and provided facilities such as tennis courts, a golf course, and a baseball park with the first electric scoreboard and night lights in the state. For seventy-five cents per month, a miner gained access to the Miners' Amusement Hall—containing ballrooms, game rooms, and clubrooms. Perhaps the ultimate service the company provided was during Prohibition when, according to author Norman Weis, it furnished premises for distilling illegal liquor.

At first, electricity was a luxury limited to

Hotel and boarding house in Madrid

a single bulb per house, but by the 1920s, unlimited electricity was available. It was during this time that the town began its spectacular Christmas displays. The celebration was an honest venture of community pride and not a commercialized Christmas exploitation, for although thousands of New Mexicans came to view the lights and cardboard figures, there were no sales of postcards and souvenirs permitted. National airlines even altered their night routes to offer a view of Madrid's dramatic lights.

The peak year of coal production was 1928, when over 180,000 tons were shipped. But as natural gas began to heat homes and diesel fuel powered locomotives, the demand for coal fell. The Christmas lights went out permanently in the early 1940s. A brief respite occurred during World War II, when the coal town of Madrid fueled the atomic city of Los Alamos. Michael Jenkinson captured the irony of the situation when he said it was like "the ewe giving suck to the wolf pup."

In 1954 the town was put up for sale for a quarter of a million dollars, but there were no takers. The town's Christmas lights were eventually sold to Gallup. In 1975 houses were sold to individuals, and the modest rebirth of Madrid began. Small crafts shops opened along the highway, and many of the company houses were renovated. But water has remained a problem since none is brought in from Waldo by rail as it was in the past. A small well pumps a mere five gallons per minute to help serve the needs of the families. Fire is a constant danger, but the volunteer fire department in nearby Cerrillos can now be summoned. In the old days, if a house caught fire, the adjacent houses were evacuated and dynamited to keep the fire from spreading.

Madrid may have lost its Christmas lights and its most dramatic building (the coal breaker), but there is still plenty to see. Dozens of company residences remain, many still unoccupied. The old Catholic church and the Miners' Amusement Hall are on the west side of town beyond a block of houses. A coal mining museum offers two steam locomotives, a tunnel, antique cars, and

Row houses in Madrid

A rusting locomotive overlooks Madrid company houses.

Madrid's Catholic church, now a private residence

Miners' amusement hall in Madrid

Golden's San Francisco Catholic Church at dawn

Cemetery at Madrid

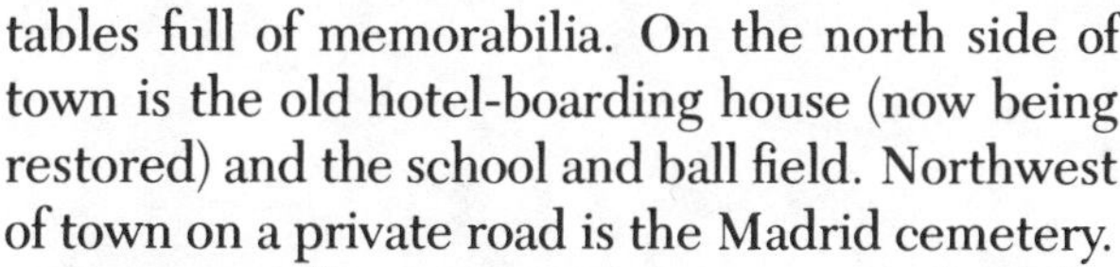

Church in Cerrillos

tables full of memorabilia. On the north side of town is the old hotel-boarding house (now being restored) and the school and ball field. Northwest of town on a private road is the Madrid cemetery.

Tourists will continue to come to Madrid despite the warning that "it is not a ghost town." It *is* one, of course, just as surely as is Bisbee, Arizona, with its hundreds of residents. For in both cases the mines are closed, many large buildings are empty, and the population is a mere whisper of what it once was. Most people do not come to these towns with a macabre curiosity to watch the dead; they come with a genuine appreciation for what is left and an honest desire to connect with what once was. Perhaps those residents of Madrid who now resent visitors will learn to accept that.

CERRILLOS

Cerrillos is 24 miles south of Santa Fe and 3 miles north of Madrid on New Mexico 14.

Los Cerrillos (the Little Hills) has been blessed with abundant minerals. It is near the site of what may have been the first mining done by western man, an open-pit turquoise effort dating from at least A.D. 500. Spaniards in the area later forced Indians to work the Mina del Tiro (Mine of the Shaft) for silver prior to the Pueblo Revolt of 1680. The first gold mining west of the Mississippi began in the nearby Ortiz Mountains in the 1820s at El Real de Dolores, also called Old Placers. So the area around Los Cerrillos, shortened by Anglos to Cerrillos, has had deposits of turquoise, silver, gold, and coal (at nearby Madrid) in abundance. The only element lacking has been water, a commodity essential for mining on any kind of scale.

The modern era of Cerrillos began in 1879, when two miners from Leadville, Colorado, found deposits of gold in the area. Shortly afterwards, the Santa Fe Railroad came through, and a post office opened in 1880. The gold fever led to discoveries of silver, copper, lead, and zinc, as well as about a million dollars' worth of turquoise. Thomas Alva Edison is said to have spent over two million dollars at his laboratory in the Ortiz Mountains trying to discover how to separate gold from its imprisoning rock through an electrostatic process because of the scarcity of water in this semiarid land. The peak of mining activity of the precious metals was over by about 1890, but by then coal was taking over as the mainstay of the economy in the area.

The population of Cerrillos once topped eight hundred, but now the town is a mere village shaded by cottonwoods near Galisteo Creek. Cerrillos contains several attractive false-front structures, a delightful church, and many adobe buildings on back streets. It also features some of

Simoni Store in Cerrillos, once the Hotel Frisco in Disney's The Nine Lives of Elfego Baca

Cemetery at Galisteo

the friendliest, most community-minded people in New Mexico. Cerrillos seems to have several centers for congregating—including the Catholic church, a bar, and the Turquoise Trail Volunteer Fire Department, of which the community is quite proud. But the genuine center seems to be the Simoni Store, housed in the large hotel building that is the showplace of the town (that honor used to belong to the Palace Hotel, now only an empty space after a devastating fire). The Simoni sisters are convivial and witty; they share the stories of Cerrillos with a pride and warmth that makes the visitor glad he asked about the town and its history. And the community spirit in Cerrillos certainly shows: when I was last there, residents were preparing a celebration for the fiftieth anniversary of the local priest's ordination—boys were sweeping sidewalks while ladies prepared an elaborate feast.

WALDO

From Cerrillos, drive north across the railroad tracks, turn left, and drive over the Devil's Throne. Waldo is just under two miles from Cerrillos.

Waldo is a very minor ghost town now—with foundations near some large cottonwoods, a few adobe homes on the hills to the south, and the crumbling ruins of coke ovens on the south side of the Santa Fe tracks.

Waldo was merely a place along the Santa Fe right-of-way until 1892, when a spur line originating there was built down to the coal mines at Madrid. Named for Henry L. Waldo, then chief justice of the New Mexico Supreme Court, the town eventually had a population of about 125. The principal industries were the ovens (built by the Colorado Fuel and Iron Company) that produced coke for smelting and the water wells that supplied Madrid with 150,000 gallons per day. Since both businesses were tied to Madrid's coal, Waldo died when the mines closed in 1954.

GALISTEO

Galisteo is 12.6 miles southeast of Cerrillos. Drive north from Cerrillos and turn right after 3.8 miles. Galisteo is 8.8 miles down a good dirt road.

Galisteo really should not be considered a ghost, but it has several attractions for those who enjoy

1882 Catholic church in Galisteo

historic old towns. Dominating the small town is the Catholic church dating from 1882. Across the street is the museum and herb store, formerly the Ortiz y Pino hacienda and still operated by a member of that family. Several adobe buildings are in disuse in the town, but most of the homes have been attractively preserved and renovated.

Originally an Indian pueblo, Galisteo was chosen in 1614 as the site for a Spanish mission. The mission was abandoned after the Pueblo Revolt of 1680, but the community was reestablished in 1702. Although the town remained small, a post office was established in 1876 and lasted until 1959.

Don't overlook the cemetery west of town. It contains a wonderful variety of gravestones, from carved wooden markers and elaborate stone statuary to primitive hand-crafted stone slabs. I consider it to be one of New Mexico's outstanding cemeteries.

GOLDEN

Golden is 11 miles south of Madrid on New Mexico 14.

Three ruined buildings in Golden; the old school is in the right foreground.

Hagan, as seen through a telephoto lens

Two adobe ruins at Coyote

El Real de San Francisco and Tuerto were two towns that developed in the 1840s as a result of placer gold deposits discovered in the San Pedro Mountains. By the 1880s the individual prospectors and small-time operators had given way to larger companies with financial and political clout. By this time Tuerto had been outdistanced by its southern neighbor, which had been renamed Golden. The gold boom was over by the mid-1880s, but ranching continued in the area. The post office closed in 1928.

Golden's most photographed building is the San Francisco Catholic Church, an attractive adobe building dating from about 1830. It was restored in 1960 by historian and author Fray Angelico Chavez. West of the church, across the highway and down in a draw, is the ruin of the stone schoolhouse.

HAGAN

Take the dirt road that heads west from the Golden Inn 2.8 miles south of Golden. Stay on the main road and take a right (north) at the only main fork. The ruins of Hagan are 10 miles from the Golden Inn.

Coal deposits found along the Uña de Gato (Cat's Claw) Arroyo brought Hagan into existence in 1902. About sixty people lived near the mine. A railroad line, the key to economical mining at the site, was not completed until 1924 after two previous spur line projects had been shelved. At this time, five hundred people lived in Hagan, and large company buildings were erected along the arroyo. In addition to coal mining, the town also depended upon cattle ranching and a brick plant. The coal seams thinned out in the early 1930s, and the town began to die. The post office closed in 1931.

The adobe and brick ruins of Hagan are posted against trespassing, but you can get a good view of the town by walking along the sandy arroyo and using a telephoto lens or binoculars. Two roofless company buildings are the principal ruins at the site.

COYOTE

Coyote is 3.2 miles northwest of Hagan.

Coyote was founded in 1904, two years after Hagan, by miners working the Sloan Mine. The prospect of a railroad spur linking the community and nearby Hagan to the Santa Fe line helped keep the town going. But townspeople watched as two rail projects died, and before the line was actually completed to Hagan in 1924, Coyote was already a ghost town. Ironically, the branch line came within one-half mile of the deserted community.

Five adobe shells, along with several foundations, still stand at the site.

LA BAJADA

About six miles north of Algodones, turn west off U.S. 85 at New Mexico 16 (*not* New Mexico 22, as it is marked on the 1977 Santo Domingo Pueblo 7½′ topographic map and other maps). Turn north after 3.5 miles, then east (right) after 1 mile at the cattleguard. At the next fork, the old townsite is to the left, and La Bajada (The Descent) Hill is to the right.

La Bajada, the community, was less well known than La Bajada, the hill. The Santa Fe Trail that linked Santa Fe and Albuquerque dropped seven hundred feet from La Bajada Mesa down to La Majada Mesa in about one mile of switchbacks and hairpins; the road was used until 1932 when the present route (U.S. 85 and I-25) was established just under four miles away.

La Bajada Mine is two miles east of town along the Santa Fe River, but it was only in operation for a few years in the 1920s. Farming was the principal occupation in the town, but in the 1940s the lure of an easier life in the nearby cities of Albuquerque and Santa Fe led to an exodus by the residents.

The building I wanted to see was a Catholic church built around 1830 that is featured in Jim and Barbara Sherman's *Ghost Towns and Mining Camps of New Mexico.* They show a photograph of the building as little more than a slumping, roofless hulk, but it has been carefully and completely restored. A few deserted adobe buildings stand nearby amid newer buildings.

CAPSULE SUMMARY

MAJOR SITES

Madrid—extensive, photogenic remains

Cerrillos—an outstanding main street

SECONDARY SITES

Golden—a beautiful restored church

Galisteo—church, buildings, and a fine cemetery

MINOR SITES

Hagan—extensive ruins, private property

Coyote—a few adobe ruins

La Bajada—restored church, deserted adobe buildings

Waldo—foundations, coke oven ruins

ROAD CONDITIONS

Coyote and Hagan—truck road that crosses many washes

All other sites—passenger car roads

TRIP SUGGESTIONS

TRIP 1: Golden, Madrid, Cerrillos

A pleasant half-day to full-day excursion from either Albuquerque or Santa Fe, this trip features the best towns in the area. Round trip distance from Santa Fe is about 80 miles; from Albuquerque, about 105 miles.

TRIP 1A: Add Galisteo to Trip 1

Going to Galisteo and back to New Mexico 14 adds 25 miles to Trip 1. Or you can take New Mexico 41 and U.S. 285 back to Santa Fe. If you do, be sure to stop in Lamy for a look at the Santa Fe depot or for a delightful dinner.

TRIP 1B: Add Waldo to Trip 1

This four-mile addition on a dirt road takes you to the area's least-preserved site.

TRIP 2: Hagan, Coyote, and La Bajada

The roughest road in the chapter is to Hagan and Coyote. Plan at least an hour for the 20-mile trip, including time spent at the sites. Then go up to U.S. 85 and head north to New Mexico 16 to La Bajada.

TRIP 2A: Combine Trip 2 with Cabezon

See Trip 1a, p. 37.

TOPOGRAPHIC MAP INFORMATION FOR CHAPTER ONE

GOLD AND COAL IN THE ORTIZ MOUNTAINS

(For map reading assistance, consult Appendix A, page 169)

Town	Topo Map Name	Size	Year	Importance*
Madrid	Madrid	15′	1961	3
Cerrillos	Madrid	15′	1961	3
Waldo	Madrid	15′	1961	3
Galisteo	Galisteo	7½′	1966	3
Golden	Madrid	15′	1961	3
Hagan	Hagan	7½′	1954	1
Coyote	Hagan	7½′	1954	1
La Bajada	Tetilla Peak	7½′	1953 (pr[a]1977)	2

[a]photo revised (see p. 172)

*1—essential to find and/or enjoy site to the fullest
2—helpful but not essential
3—unnecessary for finding and enjoying site

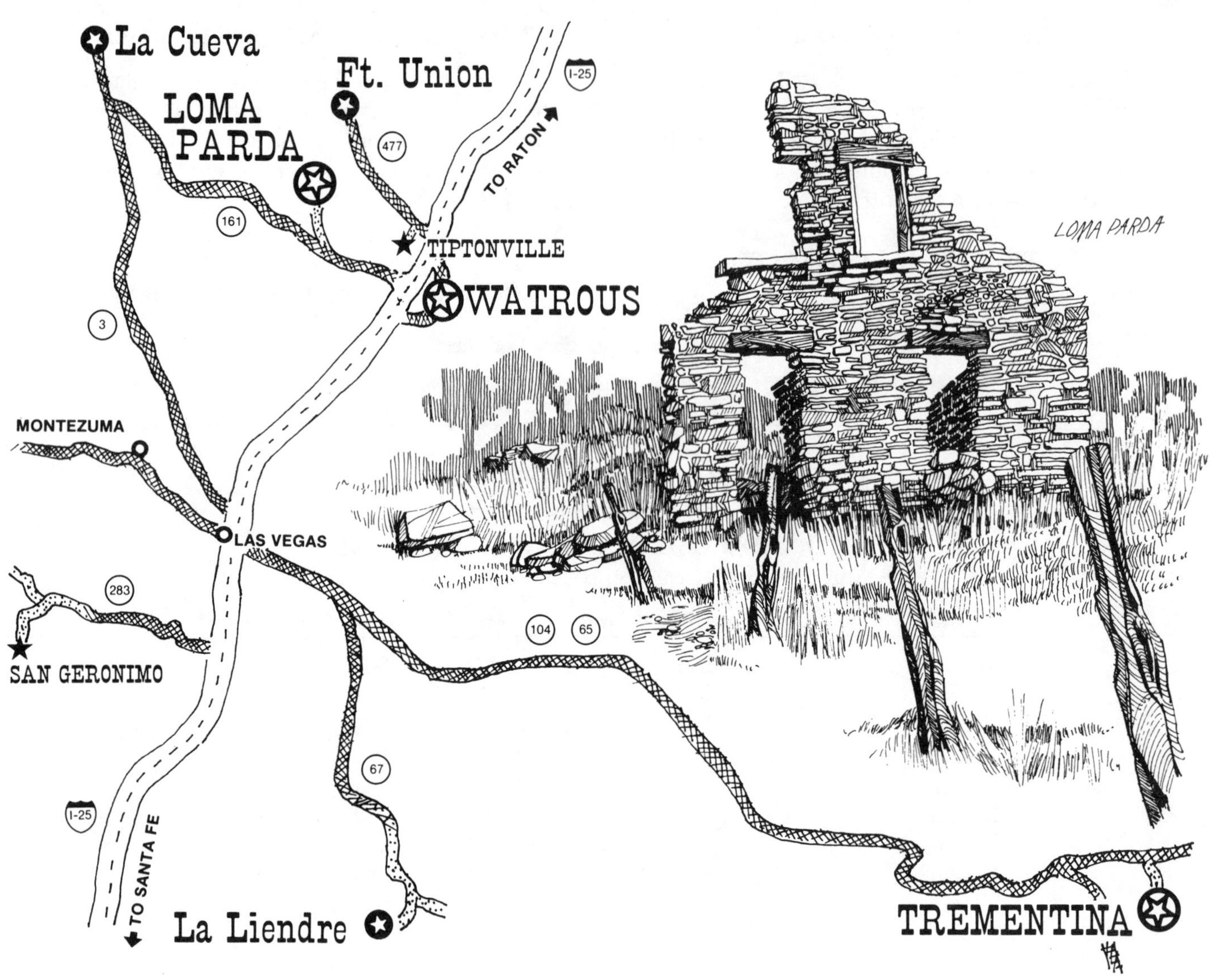
La Cueva
Ft. Union
LOMA PARDA
I-25
477
TO RATON
161
TIPTONVILLE
WATROUS
3
MONTEZUMA
LAS VEGAS
283
SAN GERONIMO
104
65
67
I-25
TO SANTA FE
La Liendre
TREMENTINA
LOMA PARDA

CHAPTER TWO

GHOSTS OF THE MEADOWS

KNOWN ORIGINALLY as Nuestra Señora de Los Dolores de Las Vegas (Our Lady of Sorrows of the Meadows), Las Vegas is one of New Mexico's most interesting, attractive, and overlooked towns. People from out of state rush to Taos and Santa Fe, which are indeed exciting places, but they are missing a great deal by zooming past Las Vegas on the interstate.

Two detailed travel guides, both written by Lynn I. Perrigo of New Mexico Highlands University, are available in Las Vegas and are extremely valuable for increasing your enjoyment of the area: "Twelve Tours" and "Historic Las Vegas." Three buildings, among dozens, that you should not neglect are the 1882 Montezuma Hotel, the 1898 Castañeda Hotel, and the 1917 railroad roundhouse.

FORT UNION

Fort Union is 8 miles north of Watrous off I-25 on New Mexico 477.

Here is a ghost town with a jail that still has cells, an adobe hospital that had thirty-six beds, Santa Fe Trail ruts that were made by wagons well over a hundred years ago, and foundations and chimneys that parade across the horizon like some western Stonehenge.

Fort Union is a ghost *fort*, not a ghost town. But it is here for two reasons. It is a wonderful national monument you shouldn't pass by; and more important to this volume, it had a distinct effect upon three communities in this chapter: Tiptonville, Watrous, and above all, Loma Parda.

Protecting travelers along the Santa Fe Trail from hostile Indians was the primary responsibility of the soldiers at Fort Union. The fort was constructed in 1851, but it is not the same structure whose ruins stand today. That fort was built after the Civil War and was occupied until 1890, when it was abandoned because the Indian threat had passed and because the arrival of the railroad in 1879 made the Santa Fe Trail obsolete.

From the 1850s to the 1880s, Fort Union's commanding officers had problems keeping their men out of trouble in the neighboring communities. There were horse races in Tiptonville, gambling saloons in Watrous, and prostitutes in Loma Parda. Because of the presence of Fort Union, Watrous became an important trading point; Tiptonville could farm in peace; and Loma Parda—well, Loma Parda would never be the same.

WATROUS

Watrous is 19 miles north of Las Vegas on I-25.

The confluence of the Mora and Sapello rivers was used as a trading point at the turn of the nineteenth century. It was called, quite simply,

The Castañeda Hotel, along the Santa Fe tracks in Las Vegas

The Montezuma Hotel, a resort from the 1880s

Part of the ruins of Fort Union

Samuel Watrous's residence and store, now the Doolittle Ranch

what it was: La Junta de Los Rios Mora y Sapello, or more concisely, La Junta. The town that eventually developed there became important as the first settlement on the western end of the Santa Fe Trail.

To La Junta in 1846 came Samuel B. Watrous, whose farm and business affairs flourished to the extent that when the railroad came through in 1879, he donated land for the right-of-way. The railroad, according to two sources, in effect changed the name of the town to Watrous by naming their rail stop in honor of the beneficent donor. Records seem to bear this out, for the official name of the town's post office changed from La Junta to Watrous in that year.

Schmidt and Reinkens General Store

Seven years later, Samuel Watrous and his son were both dead. The newspaper reports labeled both deaths as suicides, but that may well have been a cover-up. In a letter to the editor of *New Mexico Magazine,* Angeline Guerin Kramer claims that her grandmother, Belina Watrous, told her that the son had been murdered because he was his father's principal heir and that his stepmother, Josephine Chapin Watrous, had a hand in the murder, although an accomplice had actually shot him. Mrs. Kramer also reports that the senior Watrous was killed, perhaps in self-defense, by his wife Josephine during a violent domestic fight. Mrs. Kramer makes one telling point in support of her grandmother's story: the newspaper account claimed that Samuel B. Watrous, Sr., had committed suicide by shooting himself through the head twice. How, she asks logically, could someone shoot himself *twice* in the head?

The town of Watrous has many buildings to see, but six are particularly interesting. Schmidt and Reinkens general merchandise is the large white building on the main highway through town. One block west is a large livery stable that

School in Watrous

Headstone in cemetery east of the Doolittle Ranch headquarters

once was a saloon and dance hall. North on the same street, largely hidden by foliage, is the Masonic Temple, considered either the oldest or second oldest building of that order in the state. Farther down the street are the old school, standing deserted in the weeds, and across from the school, a stone church that is believed to be the oldest Protestant church in New Mexico. North on the road out of town is Samuel B. Watrous's house and store, built in 1849 or 1850, now the headquarters of the Doolittle Ranch.

As unfortunate as Samuel Watrous's end was, tragedy was not reserved for him alone. Behind the Doolittle headquarters, visible from New Mexico 97 going to Valmora, is a small cemetery hidden in grass and weeds. There five children of J. B. and L. K. Watrous are buried. Two died at less than a year old, and only two lived beyond the age of six; those two died fourteen days apart.

TIPTONVILLE

Cross I-25 at the north end of Watrous on the road to Fort Union. The turnoff to the townsite is about 1 mile up the road. Turn left and drive about 0.5 miles. The turnoff

Abandoned Masonic Temple in Watrous

Cemetery at Tiptonville

Church at La Cueva

Deserted adobe buildings at La Cueva

Trementina townsite

Julian Baca's dance hall and saloon, Loma Parda

Looking north along the back of Loma Parda's main street

to the cemetery is 0.2 miles before the road to the town.

Tiptonville, or Tipton, was a small ranching community named for the family that settled the area. William Tipton (1825–1888) was Samuel Watrous's son-in-law and one-time business partner. The town featured a post office from 1876 to 1898 and also was the site of Reverend Thomas Harwood's Methodist mission boarding school, built in 1869.

Today Tiptonville consists of about a dozen buildings, many obviously original and most occupied. It is a very pleasant setting for a ranch, but it is not much of a ghost town. The cemetery nearby is small and full of Tiptons. It is currently sinking in a bog, but it is worth a visit.

LOMA PARDA

Loma Parda is northwest of Watrous on a private ranch. The road to the site has a padlocked gate.

In 1850, Lieutenant Colonel E. V. Sumner took his first look at the U.S. troops stationed in Santa Fe and the temptations offered to soldiers there. He immediately determined to remove them from "that sink of vice and extravagance" by establishing forts only in remote areas. The plains near La Junta seemed a likely spot since the Santa Fe Trail came across there from Independence, Missouri. And, thankfully, no large towns could deter the soldiers from their duties. Loma Parda (Grey Hill), a small farming community six miles away, was the closest town.

Soldiers didn't need a town, however, to bring them some of the delights that had been available in Santa Fe. Hardly had the fort been completed in 1851 when a group of prostitutes established their trade in nearby caves. A Captain Sykes ended the sinful practice by capturing the women and shaving their heads; the caves now are a part of Cañon de Las Pelones, Baldwomen's Canyon.

But enterprising merchants in Loma Parda realized that what caves could provide, houses could provide better—or at least in more comfort. The town became what is called a "blowoff" town, where the soldiers would go to gamble, dance, drink, and carouse with women. An officer named Hollister dubbed the place "a sodom," allowing Ralph Looney, in *Haunted Highways*, to make a memorable biblical pun by calling Loma Parda "Sodom on the Mora." The Mora River did indeed run freely near Loma Parda, but it was Loma Lightning, a vicious whisky, that ran freely through the town. Hollister complained that the fort's guardhouse and hospital were filled with men who met up with the Lightning. Julian Baca's dance hall featured live music twenty-four hours a day, and the thriving bordellos gave an ironic meaning to the name of the fort.

Commanding officers tried various ploys to keep soldiers away, usually by making the town strictly off limits. The most ingenious idea considered was to lease the whole town and then destroy it. But by 1872 Loma Parda had become a town of over four hundred, with its own post office. There was at least one establishment, the McMartin brothers' mercantile, that did legitimate business with the fort itself. Mainly, however, the offerings of the town were meant for the wayward soldiers. In addition to the brothels and bars were pool halls and dance halls that served a variety of libations—even champagne. Wagon service to the fort was available for one dollar per round trip, but that was far too expensive for the average soldier.

Two stories will serve to illustrate the violence and rowdiness of Loma Parda. One night in 1882 a soldier named James Gray was murdered in town. His friends at Fort Union went AWOL dressed as cowboys and attended a dance at Loma Parda. By infiltrating and asking the right questions, they ascertained the murderer, "invited" him outside, and hanged him.

Then there was James Lafer's visit in 1888. He rode into town, hauled a woman up into the saddle with him by dragging her across his horse, and rode right into a saloon. When his horse would not drink any liquor, he summarily shot it in the head, grabbed the woman, and exited, leaving the horse dead on the barroom floor. Many other anecdotes exist about Loma Parda, the best in Looney's book and in a pamphlet called *The Loma Parda Story* by F. Stanley.

When the importance of Fort Union began to fade, so did Loma Parda. The post office lasted until 1900, or nine years after the fort was abandoned. A few families kept farming in the area, but by World War II it had been abandoned entirely. The only bridge into town washed away in 1948 and has never been replaced.

McMartin's store in Loma Parda

Directions at the beginning of this entry are deliberately sketchy. The owners of Loma Parda used to allow visitors into the site, but because of wanton vandalism, it has been closed. The church, photographed by R. P. Meleski and described by Patricia Meleski in *Echoes of the Past* as the best-preserved of the buildings, is no longer recognizable as a church. I was allowed in largely because I was writing a book that would pass along the information that the site is closed, information not given in other books that mention Loma Parda.

The town is a bit of a disappointment after seeing Meleski's and Looney's photographs. It is merely a skeleton of its former self. But a rock wall of the McMartins' store still stands, and Julian Baca's dance hall and saloon is about half under roof. Two adobe residences still could be made habitable, perhaps, and other walls and foundations line the main street. A cemetery in very poor shape is west of Baca's saloon. Even though the town is not what it was a few years ago, it is still a thrill to stand in Loma Parda, the town that gave the soldiers entertainment and the officers fits.

LA CUEVA

La Cueva is 5 miles southeast of Mora, at the junction of New Mexico 3 and 21.

Vicente Romero was supposed to have slept in caves while tending his sheep, so when he established a ranch in 1851 it seemed only natural to name it La Cueva Ranch in honor of his first home. At least that is the story.

La Cueva today really is less a town than a part of a beautiful ranch, but two buildings there, the mill and the church, are well worth seeing. La Cueva mill was built in the 1870s by Vicente Romero and operated until 1949, milling flour and generating electricity. Near the mill is the Catholic church, a sizeable adobe that still has its confessional and altar. The designs painted on the ceiling around the light fixtures are particularly attractive. A solitary grave stands beside the church, but the main cemetery is across the road.

SAN GERONIMO

Head west from I-25 on New Mexico 283, which is south of Las Vegas. After 8.5 miles, take the left fork. The San Geronimo cemetery is 1.8 miles farther west, with the townsite 0.7 miles beyond.

Perhaps San Geronimo's biggest asset is its natural beauty. From the cemetery overlooking the town, one can see the deep green trees along Tecolote Creek, the high grass of the open country, and the splendor that is the Sangre de Cristo Mountains to the west. Down along the creek is the small community of adobes that is San Geronimo.

The picturesque valley along Tecolote (Owl) Creek was settled in the mid-1830s; the town was named in honor of St. Jerome, who was a major editor of the Vulgate Bible in the fourth century. San Geronimo's most prosperous era occurred when the Santa Fe Railroad came through to Las Vegas in 1879, for the town soon became a major supplier of railroad ties.

Two dozen buildings, virtually all under roof and many of them occupied, remain. The school is now a residence, and many of the houses are a bit dilapidated, but the church's bell tower is still fresh with new paint.

A curious building technique, one I did not see elsewhere, has been used extensively in the residences of this semi-ghost: the plaster covering the adobe is scored with careful parallel lines to make the building appear to have been made of blocks rather than adobe.

San Geronimo residence

LA LIENDRE

To reach La Liendre, drive east from Las Vegas on New Mexico 65 and 104. Turn south on New Mexico 67 and go for 9.1 miles. There take the right fork. Beyond the fork 4.2 miles is the townsite. Be sure to close the stock gates you must go through.

La Liendre is one of New Mexico's most striking ghost towns. Situated on a high bank overlooking the Gallinas River, the three buildings, numerous foundations, and cemetery have both a warm beauty and an unsettling desolation. The beauty comes from the river, the dark mesas, and the rolling clouds on a summer afternoon. The desolation comes from the hard, baked ground and from the buildings themselves—two residences and a store.

La Liendre was settled in the 1840s by Spanish ranchers and was occupied well into the twentieth century. Vandals must have really decimated the town, for Betty Woods, in her pamphlet *Ghost*

La Liendre residence

Commercial building with collapsing roof at La Liendre

Towns and How to Get to Them, describes the site as having several houses, a church, and even a mailbox standing by the store. Indeed, there must have been a number of houses at one time since T. M. Pearce says that La Liendre means "a string of nits," referring to the fact that houses were strung out along the road. If there is to be a La Liendre to see in the future, visitors must treat it with much more care than they have in the past.

TREMENTINA

Take New Mexico 65 and 104 east from Las Vegas for 46 miles. Stay on 65 when 104 leaves it (at the Trementina school). See the text for further directions.

Trementina, one of New Mexico's premier ghost towns, might be called "the town that isn't there" since some maps and ghost town books overlook at least part of its ruins. The 1972 Variadero 7½′ map, for example, doesn't show anything resembling ruins at either of the sites, establishing only the location of cemeteries. Nevertheless, Trementina most assuredly *is* there.

We don't know a great deal about Trementina's early history. Farmers may have settled along the creek as early as the 1830s—and discovered a market for the pine oil and turpentine derived from the piñon trees that even today line the creek. These same farmers may have named this small stream Trementina (turpentine) Creek. Around the turn of the century, Miss Alice Blake, a Presbyterian missionary, came to Trementina. According to a visitor to Trementina in the early days, Miss Blake helped choose a second townsite, south of the creek buildings and on a higher flat mesa. There the church, a mission hospital complete with gymnasium, and several residences were built, all of the dry rock masonry also used at the original site. In 1904 the population was reported to be two hundred, and the town had a store, two saloons, and a justice of the peace; the town's postmistress, incidentally, was Alice Blake. By 1907 Miss Blake was also the Presbyterian mission school principal, and another public school was in operation.

Alice Blake retired in 1930, reportedly in ill

Trementina townsite

Trementina church

health. She was clearly the galvanizing force in the community, and her departure was the first in a series of events that began the end for Trementina. Severe droughts, the Depression, and finally enlistments during World War II depleted the population. The last resident left in 1955.

R. P. Meleski photographed Trementina only eight years later, and *Echoes of the Past* provides beautiful evidence of what the town once was but will never be again. He shows the church with the roof and steeple intact, *vigas* in place in most of the roofless buildings, and even occasional pieces of furniture. Today Trementina looks much less like a town and much more like the surrounding hills. No buildings have roofs, and the church is a hollow shell. The town still has a strong element of the ghost to it nevertheless, but it looks more like an abandoned pueblo than a missionary-inspired community.

From the Trementina school, drive 4.5 miles to the cemetery with its cut-rock wall on the north side of the road near the bridge over Trementina Creek. Many of the headstones are carved sandstone and contain hand-engraved crosses, stars, and other symbols. On the north bank of the creek are some overlooked ruins that no doubt predate the larger townsite, complete with long stone fences and buildings made of the mortarless stone walls that are Trementina's trademark. An ingenious feature of the low rock walls, which were probably for corrals, is that occasionally stones are placed vertically along the base of the wall with space between them to allow for water runoff on the mesa to pass through undisturbed to Trementina Creek.

Drive back toward the Trementina school 0.7 miles and turn south, where you will immediately cross a cattleguard. When you cross a second cattleguard, take the left fork along the barbed wire fence to the townsite, only 0.6 miles from the main road.

CAPSULE SUMMARY

MAJOR SITES

Trementina—dozens of roofless ruins at two separate sites

Watrous—explore the back streets for some of the better buildings

Loma Parda—extensive ruins but on private property closed to the public

SECONDARY SITES

Fort Union—a national monument, extensive remains with informative displays and literature

La Liendre—three buildings under roof in an enchanting setting

La Cueva—a memorable mill and church

MINOR SITES

San Geronimo—small occupied town in a lovely valley

Tiptonville—small cemetery, several buildings still in use

ROAD CONDITIONS

La Liendre—a truck road

Trementina—a truck road to the southern site, but a passenger car could make it part way—with a short walk to the site

Loma Parda—rough truck road but closed to the public

All other sites—passenger car roads

TRIP SUGGESTIONS

TRIP 1: Watrous, Tiptonville, Fort Union

You'll probably want to spend 1½–2 hours at both Watrous and Fort Union, so allow 5–6 hours for this 60-mile round trip from Las Vegas.

TRIP 1A: Add La Cueva to Trip 1

Instead of returning to Las Vegas via I-25, make a scenic, historic loop by taking New Mexico 161 through Las Golondrinas to La Cueva. Total distance round trip from Las Vegas: 93 miles.

TRIP 2: San Geronimo

Plan to spend 1½–2 hours for this 30-mile trip.

TRIP 3: La Liendre and Trementina

You'll need a truck and at least one-half day to make this 125-mile trip from Las Vegas. If you take a passenger car, go only to Trementina and cut 25 miles and two hours from your trip.

TRIP 3A: Combine Trip 3 with towns in Chapter Five.

See Trip Suggestions, p. 67, for possibilities. You can create an interesting loop trip back to Las Vegas.

TOPOGRAPHIC MAP INFORMATION FOR CHAPTER TWO

GHOSTS OF THE MEADOWS

(For map reading assistance, consult Appendix A, page 169)

Town	Topo Map Name	Size	Year	Importance*
Fort Union	Fort Union	7½′	1963	3
Watrous	Watrous	7½′	1966	3
Tiptonville	Watrous	7½′	1966	2
Loma Parda	Loma Parda	7½′	1963	1
La Cueva	Rainsville	7½′	1963	3
San Geronimo	San Geronimo	7½′	1961	3
La Liendre	Apache Springs	15′	1960	2
Trementina	Variadero	7½′	1972	2

*1—essential to find and/or enjoy site to the fullest
2—helpful but not essential
3—unnecessary for finding and enjoying site

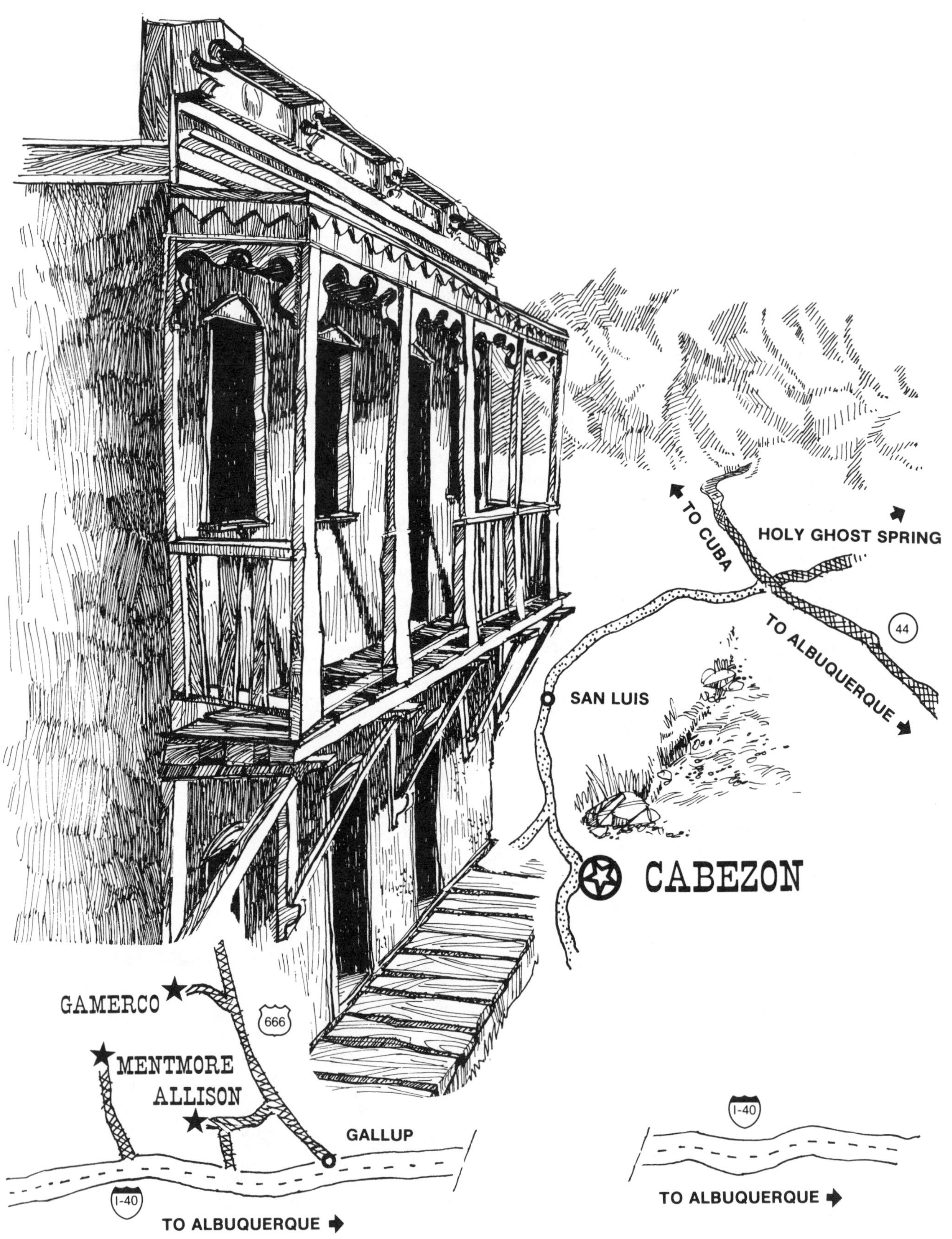

TO CUBA
HOLY GHOST SPRING
44
TO ALBUQUERQUE
SAN LUIS
CABEZON
GAMERCO
666
MENTMORE
ALLISON
GALLUP
I-40
TO ALBUQUERQUE
I-40
TO ALBUQUERQUE

CHAPTER THREE

CABEZON AND THE GHOSTS OF GALLUP

THERE MAY BE DOZENS of reasons to go to Gallup, but the ghost towns there, quite frankly, are not reason enough to make the trip. Cabezon, however, is a different matter. Located northwest of Albuquerque off the road to Cuba, Cabezon is very special—if you can get in to see it.

CABEZON

Drive 42 miles northwest from Bernalillo on New Mexico 44 to an intersection. Turn left (Holy Ghost Spring is marked to the right), go through the town of San Luis and across a clearly marked gas line. 2.2 miles beyond the gas line, take the left fork. The gate to the townsite is 0.5 miles beyond the fork.

Mogollon has more spectacular scenery, Madrid has more buildings, and Koehler is even more deserted. But Cabezon has the most outstanding combination of all these ingredients: I consider it New Mexico's best ghost town. Part of its enchantment is the difficulty involved in seeing it. You must drive a considerable distance from anything resembling a large town; the country is barren and, in summer, quite hot; and getting in to photograph the site can be a chancy and even hazardous proposition.

The Navajo called the magnificent volcanic plug that rises seventeen hundred feet above the Rio Puerco "the Giant's Head," from a legend that told of the Twin War Brothers killing a giant on what is now called Mt. Taylor. His spilled blood accounted for the lava beds at Grants, and his head came to rest some forty miles east. The Spaniards who came to farm the area around 1767 acknowledged the Navajo legend when they named the peak Cabezon, "the big head." The Navajo, however, considered the Spaniards intruders since the peak had traditionally marked the eastern boundary of their territory. They managed to chase most of the interlopers out and keep them out until 1826; it was not until 1863 that the U.S. Army, led by Kit Carson, finally made the area safe for farming and ranching.

Eventually La Posta, as the community was then called, became a stop for fresh horses along a stage route from Santa Fe to Fort Wingate and finally all the way to Prescott, Arizona. In 1891, when a post office was granted, the name of the town was officially changed to Cabezon.

John Pflueger and Richard F. Heller came to Cabezon in 1888 to run a general store. Heller eventually bought out his partner and became the most important resident in the history of the town. He was well known for his generosity and hospitality in a community that was just as well known for its reluctance to accept outsiders. Heller became prosperous, owning an estimated

Richard Heller's store and a movie set building

Church and cemetery at Cabezon

Original adobe structure with movie set addition; Cabezon Peak in the background

Adobe building with Cabezon Peak in background

Richard Heller's store in Cabezon. Note cotes and perches for pigeons above porch roof.

Headframe, company building, and stack at Gamerco

two thousand cattle and ten thousand sheep in addition to his mercantile business. One source says that it was not uncommon for forty wagons to be used to haul Heller's wool to market in Albuquerque. In 1894 he was instrumental in the construction of the most prominent building in town, La Iglesia de San Jose; the church still stands as one of the better-preserved buildings.

By 1920 Cabezon was a community of about 250, with the church, four stores, several dance halls, a post office, bars and, among the dozens of homes, Heller's eleven-room house that was the town's showplace. Then the downhill slide began.

The Santa Fe Railroad decided against a branch through Cabezon, depriving the town of benefits that might have given it permanence. In 1934 the U.S. Government purchased the Ojo del Espiritu Santo (Holy Ghost Spring) Land Grant, bringing the badly overgrazed and eroded land near Cabezon under strict land management control. That dealt a severe blow to the cattle ranchers. Then, in the early 1940s, a rampaging Rio Puerco burst the dams that had been made by farmers, effectively wiping out agriculture along the river. In 1947, Richard Heller, the stable force in the community for almost sixty years, died. His widow kept the post office open for over a year after his death, but then she moved to Albuquerque, and the post office closed. Within a couple of years the town had been abandoned.

The road into Cabezon is barred by a locked gate. A sign promises a stiff fine and prosecution for entering. Part of the town is visible from the gate, and a good view is available from a low mesa north of the site. I decided to pass the "no trespassing" sign and walk into town, without a camera, to ask permission to photograph, hoping that the worst I would get would be a refusal and an order to get off the property. It was not easy to leave my camera behind and then to walk along a deserted street with about two dozen buildings, most of which are photographic delights. After a lengthy conversation with a woman who was a part of one of the two families still living in the town, I was given cautious permission to photograph if I did not enter any buildings, if I stayed on the main street, and if I passed along this message: Cabezon has been carved and pillaged, and the people there are, understandably, angry and resentful about it. They have caught people breaking every window in town, tearing up floorboards in the church, and attempting to desecrate graves. The woman I talked to was very pleasant after we had time to become acquainted, but bitter experiences have made her and her husband naturally suspicious and even hostile towards strangers.

So if you are determined to see Cabezon, know that you may not be allowed in. If you decide to violate the "no trespassing" sign, be prepared for the possible consequences. But I would say this: going in without a camera and walking down the main road and asking permission of Mr. or Mrs. Lucero worked for me and is certainly preferable to sneaking in and attempting to examine the place.

If you are allowed in, be sure to notice Heller's store, the third building from the end on the north side, and his house directly across the street. Two doors down from the store is a building almost too photogenic to be real, and it isn't; it was built for the film *My Name is Nobody.* The San Jose Church and a dozen or more other buildings will keep your camera busy. And so will the presence in the background of Cabezon Peak, the Giant's Head.

GAMERCO

Take U.S. 666 for 2.5 miles north of Gallup and turn left at the Gamerco sign.

Gamerco, an acronym for the parent Gallup American Coal Company, was established in 1922, two years after coal mining operations had begun in the area. The town seemed to be ideal: working conditions were as safe as possible, salaries were good, and hours were not long. The miners were so contented that they rejected opportunities to unionize.

Gamerco is a ghost town only in the sense that its coal mines—the original reason for founding a town—have shut down; the power plant, headframe, coal chutes, and company office all stand idle. But the town itself is quite alive. The company houses and apartments are occupied, and a new shopping center has been built just north of the old mine.

ALLISON

Returning toward Gallup from Gamerco, turn west on the road just north of the

Remnants of coal operation at Mentmore

interstate interchange. Turn right again at the stop sign. The townsite is 1.6 miles from that intersection.

Allison looks even less like a ghost town than does Gamerco. Several dwellings, most of them apparently renovated, appear to be original buildings of the coal town that existed from 1913 until the mid-thirties. Unlike Gamerco, there is nothing as dramatic as a giant smokestack or headframe.

Allison was named for the coal property's third owner, Fletcher J. Allison, who acquired the mines in 1897 as an official of the Victor American Coal Company. The town had a peak population of about five hundred and as at Gamerco, the company made a substantial effort to keep employees happy—with free water, free electricity, and amenities like a tennis court.

MENTMORE

From Allison, drive south to U.S. 66. Turn west and drive 2.2 miles to a turnoff north (signs are for Mentmore Meadows and the Mentmore Mission). The townsite is 0.6 miles north of the intersection.

The town of Dilco, a loose acronym for the parent company, was created when the Direct Coal Company began mining west of Gallup in 1913. Five years later the property and operations changed ownership; the town's name went to Mentmore, and the company became the Defiance Coal Company. The mines remained open until 1952. During these years, the town reached a peak population of five hundred.

The Gallup West 7½′ map, drawn in 1963 and photorevised in 1979 for the new interstate, shows a small row of company houses remaining, but all except one are gone. A church and a general merchandise store provide the life in Mentmore today. The road north to the Carbon City Mine is private and closed, but you can see an old coal chute abandoned on the east side of the road. The Defiance Coal Company has even left its mark on the topographic map: west of town, along the Santa Fe tracks, is Defiance Draw.

CAPSULE SUMMARY

MAJOR SITE

Cabezon—one of the West's top ghost towns, but closed to the public

MINOR SITES

Gamerco—occupied company houses, some deserted mine buildings

Allison—several occupied buildings

Mentmore—one occupied company house and a general store

ROAD CONDITIONS

Cabezon—dirt road, but certainly passable for passenger cars

Other sites—paved roads

TRIP SUGGESTIONS

TRIP 1: Cabezon

Cabezon is 150 miles round trip from Albuquerque and 200 from Santa Fe. If you can gain access to the site, plan on at least an hour there.

TRIP 1A: Combine Cabezon with trips in Chapter One

A trip to Hagan, Coyote, and La Bajada (see Trip 2, p. 13), for example, could easily be combined with a drive to Cabezon. Plan for a full day.

TRIP 2: Gamerco, Allison, and Mentmore

Gallup is 131 miles from Albuquerque. Plan on about seven hours, almost five of which will be spent on the road.

TOPOGRAPHIC MAP INFORMATION FOR CHAPTER THREE

CABEZON AND THE GHOSTS OF GALLUP

(For map reading assistance, consult Appendix A, page 169)

Town	Topo Map Name	Size	Year	Importance*
Cabezon	San Luis	7½′	1961	2
Gamerco	Gallup West	7½′	1963 (pr[a]1979)	3
Allison	Gallup West	7½′	1963 (pr[a]1979)	3
Mentmore	Gallup West	7½′	1963 (pr[a]1979)	2

[a]photo revised (see p. 172)

*1—essential to find and/or enjoy site to the fullest
2—helpful but not essential
3—unnecessary for finding and enjoying site

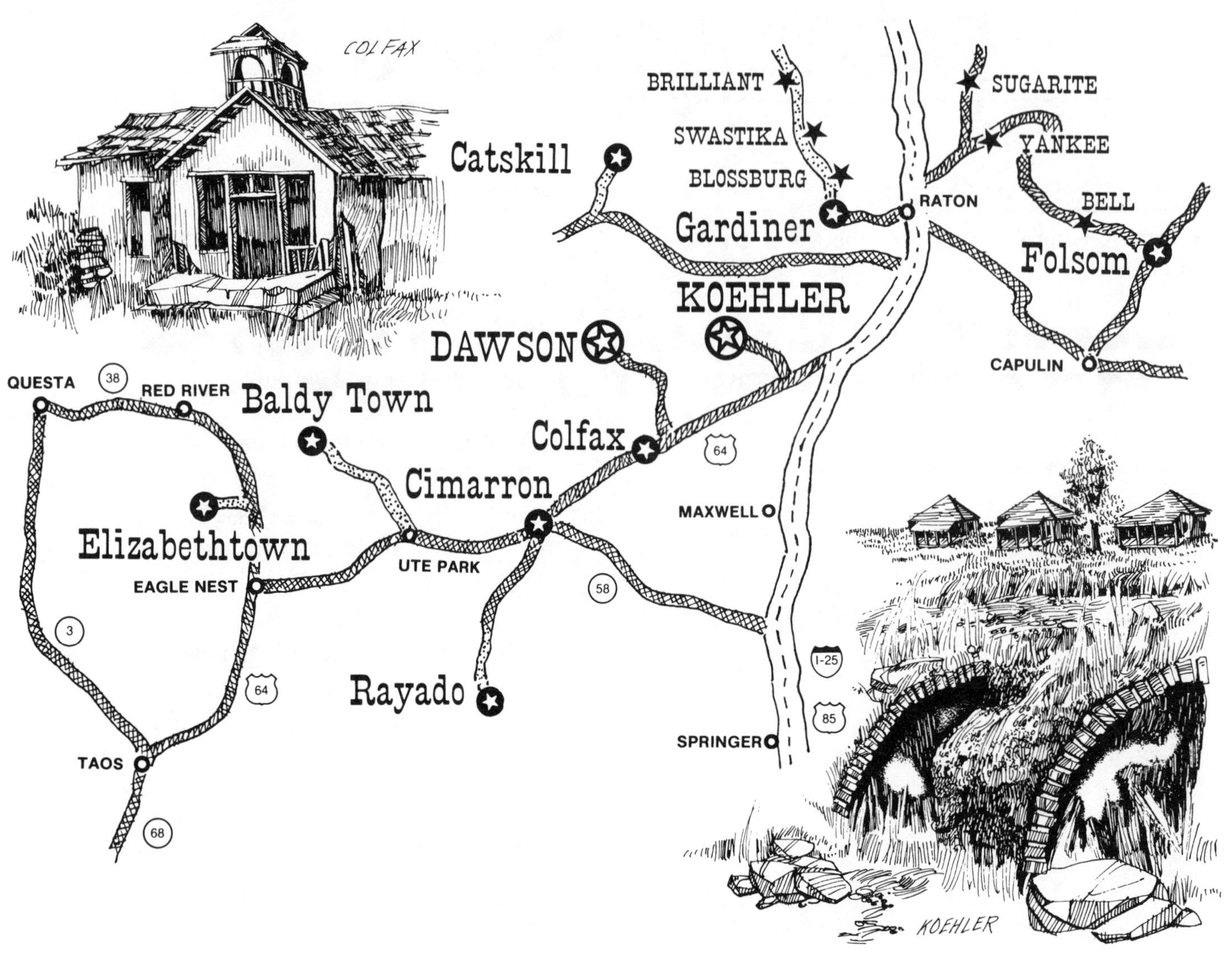
COLFAX
Catskill
BRILLIANT
SWASTIKA
BLOSSBURG
Gardiner
SUGARITE
YANKEE
RATON
BELL
Folsom
KOEHLER
DAWSON
CAPULIN
QUESTA
38
RED RIVER
Baldy Town
Colfax
64
Cimarron
Elizabethtown
MAXWELL
UTE PARK
EAGLE NEST
58
3
I-25
64
Rayado
85
SPRINGER
TAOS
68
KOEHLER

CHAPTER FOUR

COLFAX COUNTY: TOWNS OF THE HIGH COUNTRY

TAOS IS A MARVELOUS PLACE. The only problem is that everyone else knows it, too, so the town becomes stiflingly crowded during the summer. In the midst of the crush, however, I found solitude at Kit Carson's grave, a spot you shouldn't miss.

In Chapter Two I mentioned Las Vegas as an overlooked town. Raton, an attractive, friendly, and historically interesting community, is another such place. It is also surrounded by excellent ghost towns; unfortunately, most of the best are behind locked gates and "no trespassing" signs. In fact, of the sixteen sites in this chapter, you cannot visit eight without first securing someone's permission. Check individual entries for particulars.

ELIZABETHTOWN

Drive north 4.8 miles from Eagle Nest on New Mexico 38 and turn left onto the dirt road. The buildings and remains of Elizabethtown are only 0.3 miles from the turnoff.

The amount written about Elizabethtown is just about inversely proportional to what is left at the site. More differing versions exist about the origins, daily life, and tales of this once-roaring camp than any other I have researched in New Mexico. But for all the volumes, fewer than one-half dozen original buildings remain—along with a cemetery. That is not to imply, though, that visiting Elizabethtown is a disappointment; one ruin is quite photogenic, and the surrounding landscape might just place the town in New Mexico's most gorgeous valley, with Baldy Mountain (12,441 feet) and Wheeler Peak (the state's highest at 13,161 feet) as eastern and western sentinels.

A wounded Indian, rescued in 1866 by soldier John William Moore and taken to Fort Union to recover, showed his gratitude by bestowing upon Moore some "pretty rocks" which Moore recognized as copper-bearing. Guided to Baldy Mountain, the source of the rocks, Moore and others found copper, all right, but it was the placer deposits of gold found first in Willow Creek and subsequently practically everywhere else that brought a rush to the Moreno Valley. The land was a part of the Maxwell Land Grant (see Cimarron and Rayado entry, p. 44), and Lucien Maxwell, entrepreneur that he was, entered into the mining business himself, joining the Copper Mining Company in 1867. Maxwell also constructed a good road to the area and then charged others a toll to use it.

John Moore and other miners and businessmen platted a townsite in 1868 and incorporated it (the first in New Mexico) as Elizabethtown, named after Moore's daughter Elizabeth. Popular versions of the story claim she was the first baby

Stone ruin at Elizabethtown

born near the townsite, but Ralph Looney reports that Elizabeth Caterina Moore was actually born in 1863, three years before the Moreno Valley boom began. A post office opened in that first year, and by year's end the population, according to various sources, was either 3,000 or 5,000 or 7,000—take your pick. By 1869 Elizabethtown, quickly shortened by miners to "E-town," featured a reported one hundred buildings, including two hotels, three dance halls, a drugstore, five stores, and seven saloons; the saloons, some of which were one hundred to two hundred feet long, boasted dance floors and gaming tables in addition to bars. In 1870 Elizabethtown became the first county seat of newly established Colfax County, but within two years the seat was moved to Cimarron.

Finding adequate supplies of water for placer mining and milling in Moreno Valley posed genuine problems for the town's citizens. Therefore, plans were made soon after the town's founding for a remarkable water project known as the Big Ditch. An engineering marvel for the time, the Big Ditch diverted water from the Red River through ditches and pipes over trestles, along canyons, and through siphons for a distance of forty miles at a cost of $280,000. Although it did not initially bring in as much water as hoped and required constant maintenance, the Big Ditch was in use until 1900.

Elizabethtown's most sensational and grisliest crime story broke in the fall of 1870. A sobbing, bleeding Ute Indian woman burst into an E-town saloon with a story that would make today's yellow journalists salivate. She choked out how her husband, Charles Kennedy, had been systematically luring travelers, perhaps as many as fourteen in all, into his cabin south of town, on the road to Taos, and then murdering them (one version of the story says that he had even killed two of his own children when they displeased him). On this particular night she had witnessed

Commercial building, possibly Froelick's store, at Elizabethtown

another passerby enticed inside. According to Ralph Looney's version of the tale, the visitor asked Kennedy if there were any Indians around, and Kennedy's (remaining) son queried, "Can't you smell the one Papa put under the floor?"

Kennedy went into a titanic rage, shooting his guest and bashing his son's head against the fireplace; then he threw both bodies into the cellar, locked his wife in the house, and drank himself into a stupor. Understandably terrified for her own safety, the woman climbed up through the chimney and escaped to town to tell her story.

Kennedy was seized that night, and the mob did in fact find human bones in the house. A skull was subsequently found nearby and a witness to one murder came forth. Townspeople demanded the immediate "justice" so often found in the Old West, and Kennedy was put in a noose and dragged to his death through the streets of Elizabethtown.

Two grim versions provide the denouement to the Kennedy story: one says that his skeleton was wired together and sent to the Smithsonian for study, as Kennedy's skull was "peculiar." Another version states that Kennedy's corpse was decapitated and the head was presented to Henry (Henri) Lambert, once a cook to Grant and Lincoln, formerly an Elizabethtown hosteler, and at that time proprietor of the well-known St. James in Cimarron. Lambert was ordered to hang it outside as a grisly reminder to those who would consider such evil acts. The head stayed so long on the corral fence that it mummified.

Apparently, vigilante action was fairly common in E-town. On one occasion a Mexican was granted a change of venue because of the seething feeling about him in Elizabethtown. The accused was taken from the sheriff and hanged. Pinned to his corpse was a note: "So much for change of venue."

Elizabethtown was a virtual ghost in 1875, only seven years after its incorporation. But it came

Wooden markers at the E-town cemetery

back dramatically in the 1890s because of a different kind of gold mining: dredging. In 1901, a monstrous dredge, christened the *Eleanor*, was hauled piece by piece from the railhead at Springer. In its first year of operation, the giant paid for itself and cleared $100,000, mining a remarkable one-quarter of all the gold found in New Mexico that year in the process.

A fire that started in Remsberg's store in 1903 devastated the town. The dredging operation died in 1905, and *Eleanor* was left to sink into the sands of Moreno Creek. There was one last attempt at life during World War I, but the prosperity was over. The post office closed in 1931, and all mining activity eased with the advent of World War II. The Moreno Valley had produced five million dollars in gold in seventy-five years—most of it in the first forty.

The cemetery on the hill just north of town looks down on what is left of Elizabethtown: a few residences, at least two of which are originals, and two commercial buildings. One wooden structure, now modified, may originally have been Froelick's store, which survived the 1903 fire. There are several possibilities for the other building, a two-story stone beauty. Jim and Barbara Sherman say it was Remsberg's store (but there is no evidence of a fire's starting in it, and it was rather large for a store, with two stories and a full attic); *New Mexico Magazine*'s pamphlet *Listen to the Wind* claims it was the Mutz Hotel (but others say the Mutz was wooden and was destroyed in later years). *Sunset's* book *Ghost Towns of the West* calls it the town hall (but a photograph of the site in 1890 shows the complete building, and it has a commercial look to it). Ralph Looney describes it as another hotel—not the Mutz.

Ofelia Barber, now in her seventies and living in Sallisaw, Oklahoma, remembers the two-story stone ruin well. She moved to Elizabethtown prior to 1920 and lived in the ground floor of the building, which then had rooms for rent on the first floor and a dance hall on the second. She has fond memories of the dance hall, for it was there that she was married in 1927. But other memories of Elizabethtown are not so fond. Mrs. Barber left the community for good in 1936, leaving behind a husband and two daughters in the Elizabethtown Cemetery.

BALDY TOWN

Baldy Town is 7.3 miles northwest of Ute Park (12 miles east of Eagle Nest) on private property. The road is marked as the one to Ute Creek Ranch.

Just a few minutes' flight for an eagle from Elizabethtown is Baldy Town (or Baldy, or Baldy Camp), but the way is considerably longer for us terrestrials.

The first strikes that brought Elizabethtown prosperity were on the side of Baldy Mountain, the 12,441-foot peak with the treeless face. In 1866 the Mystic Lode copper mine was staked, but gold placers along Willow Creek made copper a forgotten mineral. The Aztec Lode mine, worked first in 1868, became the richest find, producing over four million dollars in gold. The most ambitious project to root out Baldy's treasure was a tunnel that was begun in 1900 and completed thirty-six years later as miners searched in vain for the peak's mother lode.

Baldy Town had a peak population of around two hundred, and the post office lasted from 1888 to 1926. Most of the buildings were razed in 1948. The town and ten thousand surrounding acres were donated anonymously to the Philmont

Placer evidence along Ute Creek

Miner's cabin at Baldy Town

Boy Scout Ranch with headquarters near Rayado (see below) in 1963. A road to the town is county property, but the site itself is private, and visitors without authorization are not permitted on the premises. All a person can see along the county road is extensive evidence of placer mining in Ute Creek, 4.9 miles from U.S. 64; the Jackson cemetery (on private property); and the mill foundations at Baldy Town.

Having received permission to photograph Baldy Town, I left my truck at a locked barrier across the road a short distance from the townsite. The rock building that appears on page 11 in the Shermans' *Ghost Towns and Mining Camps of New Mexico* is now merely a low foundation, so I was prepared for disappointment. But Boy Scout Charles Ketcham, spending his third summer at Baldy Town, led me off on an exhilarating (especially at ten thousand feet) hike to show what he had discovered in the area. We found five cabins, two still under roof, scattered through the dense growth. The most elaborate one was a stone residence with a back door serving as the entrance to a collapsed adit. A friend who accompanied me peered into the darkness of one cabin only to see a startled buck charging him. The buck wasn't the only one startled. Most of the cabins are near the Bull of the Woods Mine, but scouts have hiking paths up to French Henry Mine and others. The donor who made such a generous gift to the Boy Scouts should see the joy, enthusiasm, and energy in the scouts I saw up at Baldy Town. He would be well repaid for his beneficence.

CIMARRON AND RAYADO

Cimarron is 40 miles southwest of Raton and 57 miles east of Taos on U.S. 64. Rayado is about 11 miles south of Cimarron on New Mexico 21.

Cimarron and Rayado are historic places, not ghost towns at all, but they are included here because both towns are inextricably a part of the lives of two of New Mexico's most important people, Lucien Bonaparte Maxwell and Kit Carson.

Carson, who came to New Mexico in 1826, started a ranch on Rayado Creek in 1845 when he was only twenty-six. Lucien Maxwell came four years later to build a ranch near his friend Carson. Maxwell had married Luz Beaubien, daughter of wealthy landowner Carlos Beaubien, in 1842. Beaubien was one of the two holders of the enormous Beaubien-Miranda Land Grant. Maxwell eventually bought out Miranda's share of the grant and inherited the other half, becoming in the process the owner of the largest single tract of land ever possessed by one man in the history of the United States—over 1.7 million acres.

The St. James Hotel (now the Don Diego) in Cimarron, once run by famous chef Henry Lambert

A reconstruction of Carson's home and the original Maxwell home stand in Rayado today, along with the attractive Chapel of the Holy Child. The buildings are part of the vast Philmont Ranch owned by the Boy Scouts of America.

Cimarron was settled in 1841, the year of the origin of the Beaubien-Miranda Land Grant, and became an important stop on the Santa Fe Trail twenty years later. Lucien Maxwell moved from Rayado to Cimarron (a word generally used to describe something wild or unruly) in the late 1850s, and when a post office was granted in 1861, Maxwell was the first postmaster. He built an enormous home, no longer standing, that was a showplace residence of the West. Maxwell sold his land empire in 1869, retiring to Fort Sumner, where he died in 1875. He is buried about five miles southeast of the town of Fort Sumner near the site of the old fort. It is ironic that most people travel to the cemetery to see the grave of someone else: for as important as Lucien Maxwell was to the history of New Mexico, he is buried near the grave of a notorious kid, William Bonney (see Chapter Six, page 69).

Colfax townsite, looking from the schoolyard

Of interest in Cimarron today are a few buildings south of the main highway. Prominent among them are the Don Diego Hotel, formerly the St. James; an old garage, once Swink's Gambling Hall; and the three-story gray stone grist mill, now a museum, built in 1864 by Lucien Maxwell.

COLFAX

Colfax is 28 miles southwest of Raton and 13 miles northeast of Cimarron on U.S. 64.

New Mexico has mining ghosts, railroad ghosts, military ghosts, farming ghosts, and even mineral water ghosts, but Colfax is the only "land promoter's ghost" that I know of.

Colfax County was created in 1869 and named for the then vice-president of the United States. The town of Colfax was promoted by developers of the St. Louis, Rocky Mountain and Pacific Railroad near the turn of the century. They advertised Colfax as a good farming opportunity that was close to Cimarron and, more importantly, the expanding coal operations at Dawson. A post office opened in 1908. Although a modest community with a school, a church, a hotel, a general merchandise, and a gas station survived into the thirties, the post office closed in 1921. Apparently the town was simply too near Dawson and Cimarron to keep its own identity. Land promoters, however, have sporadically attempted to sell the place again and again, despite pretty good evidence that the town is dead. Perhaps the interest Kaiser Steel has shown in the coal in York Canyon will perk up the land agents and have them scurrying for Colfax once more.

At least four books exhibit the two-story Colfax Hotel (also once known as the Dickman Hotel). Norman Weis featured the building on the cover of *Helldorados, Ghosts and Camps of the Old Southwest*. The hotel, alas, is gone, and others in the small town are faring badly. The only structure really holding up well at all is the 1909 schoolhouse, closed since 1939, that also served as a church. It is also the only building more than a few yards off the main highway. Perhaps there is a cause-and-effect relationship here as to why it

1909 Colfax school

is still standing. A few foundations, walls, and a couple of railroad cars (one a fine passenger coach) comprise the rest of the site.

DAWSON

From Colfax, drive across the bridge toward Raton and turn left. The locked gate into Dawson is 4.5 miles from the highway. The cemetery is 0.2 miles from the locked gate back around to the right. It is open to the public.

You will never forget it. Standing in the dried grass are crosses, some with no names. Occasionally an individualized cross supplements the small one, and its message, in one of several languages, says the same thing as the others: "Emmanuel G. Minotakis, died Oct. 1913 in mine explosion" and "Vincenzo Di Lorenzo . . . Morto Nell' Esplosione 8 Febb. 1923."

Dawson, New Mexico, was to be the ideal company town. It featured schools, a theater, a bowling alley, a modern hospital, a golf course, and even an opera house. Miners from countries like Greece, Italy, China, Ireland, and Mexico worked together to dig the coal that fueled an area equal to one-sixth of the United States. And yet it was as though Dawson had been born under a bad sign.

J. B. Dawson purchased a piece of the Maxwell Land Grant in 1867 for $3,700. He thought he had obtained approximately one thousand acres, but it turned out to be a parcel of over twenty thousand acres. Dawson supplemented his ranching income by selling coal to his neighbors since a nearby seam more than provided for his needs. In 1901 he sold his property for $400,000 to the Dawson Fuel Company, who a few years later sold it to Phelps Dodge. This was the company that determined to make Dawson an ideal coal town by providing the previously mentioned amenities. At one time, nine thousand people lived in Dawson, and its future seemed extremely promising.

Then, on October 22, 1913, an incorrectly set dynamite charge resulted in an enormous explosion in Stag Cañon Mine No. 2 that sent a tongue of fire one hundred feet out of the tunnel mouth. Rescue efforts were well organized and exhaustive; Phelps Dodge sent a trainload of doctors,

Mule barn at Dawson

Dawson service station

Empty house on a Dawson residential street. Note power house, stack, and coke ovens.

Ruins of over five dozen coke ovens, with power house and stacks at Dawson

nurses, and medical supplies up from El Paso; and striking miners in Colorado ceased picketing and offered to form rescue teams. But there was little need for anything except caskets. Only a few miners escaped, and 263 died in one of the worst mining disasters in the history of the United States. The dead were buried in a special section of the cemetery, each with a small iron cross.

Almost ten years later, a mine train jumped its track, hit the supporting timbers of the tunnel mouth, and ignited coal dust in the mine. Although it was not the same shaft as before, the effect was horrifyingly similar. Many women who lost husbands in the earlier disaster waited anxiously for their sons to appear out of the smoke. But 123 more men perished in February of 1923, and the crosses in the special section then numbered 385.

Ghost town enthusiasts love to wander about mills, peer down shafts, and browse through cabins; and I think that it is rather easy to romanticize the lives of the men who worked the mines or at least to feel rather detached about them as individuals. It's as if we are less concerned with their lives than their leavings. A trip to the Dawson cemetery, then, should be obligatory, for we can see the importance and the value of their lives as it is mirrored by their graves. It is a hard person who is not deeply moved by the sight.

The cemetery at Dawson is the only part of the town open to the visitor. The townsite is again part of a working ranch, just as it was prior to 1901. Not too much remains, anyway. When Phelps Dodge closed the mines in 1950 because oil and natural gas had taken over the energy market, they put the town's buildings up for sale complete or for scrap. The giant coal washer was shipped piece by piece to Kentucky; several houses were moved out and relocated; a Phoenix firm dismantled much of the town for salvage; the safe ended up in the Phelps Dodge headquarters in Bisbee, Arizona, and is now displayed at the mining museum there. Dawson had attracted miners from all over the world, and it seems that Dawson, in turn, was spread over about half of it.

That is not to say nothing remains. I have twice taken the ten-minute walk into town to ask permission to photograph there, and twice it has been granted. As is so often the case, asking should precede the taking of even one photograph, as difficult as that can be to do (see Cabezon, page 31). The first building is the Conoco service station, featuring N-tane for thirty-one cents per gallon. The large gray building on the left is the mule barn, where the animals were housed when they were brought out of the mines once a month. A few residences and buildings around the barn are used by the ranch. On the street to the northeast are two homes, one occupied, with sidewalks along the road and concrete steps leading up to a vacant knoll. A short distance away are the dominant remains of Dawson—the coke ovens, chimneys, and power house. One street to the west has a house that still looks quite habitable, but its windows are boarded, and the front porch swing needs some attention. The danger in Dawson now is not mine explosions but rattlesnakes; I was provided a long stick for my walk through town since three had been found recently.

The cemetery at Dawson with its iron crosses

The fact most difficult to grasp at this pleasant, grassy ranch is that it was a town of over nine thousand people. It had championship football teams. People emigrated from their homes in Europe and Asia to come here. And 385 of them died in two moments of horror.

KOEHLER

The padlocked gate at the turnoff to Koehler is 16 miles southwest of Raton on U.S. 64. The townsite is 4.7 miles from the gate on private property.

Koehler is one of a kind in New Mexico, for it is the only site with considerable remains in

Koehler—main street and company houses

relatively habitable condition that is absolutely deserted. The town's condition can be credited to Kaiser Steel, who years ago padlocked the gate across the only road into town, thus sparing Koehler much of the casual, senseless vandalism so common at other sites—notably Loma Parda.

Mr. Nick Yaksich, assistant to the manager at Kaiser Steel's York Canyon Coal Mine, questioned me in a thorough but friendly way about my request to photograph Kaiser's six ghost towns in the Raton area. It became evident that Kaiser and Mr. Yaksich frequently must refuse such requests; they have only to look at what vandals have done despite their precautions (see Catskill entry, p. 51) to estimate what could be done if sites were readily visitable. I was granted access to the sites partly because I assured Mr. Yaksich that I would make clear something not mentioned in other books: Koehler and the sites in the following two entries are private property and are not open to the public.

If it were not for the padlocked gate, a tourist could turn off U.S. 64 onto a good blacktop road and, after almost five miles, enter something out of an old Alfred Hitchcock movie. I received the eerie feeling, as I entered Koehler near sunset, that the residents had been drawn out of a quiet, pleasant town—almost as if they were up there in the hills, looking down at the lone intruder. Holden Caulfield said the movies can ruin you.

Deserted house at Koehler

Charcoal ovens at Catskill

Eight identical company houses constructed of compressed coke breeze, a by-product of the coke ovens, line the north side of the highway entering town through Prairie Crow Canyon. The faded double yellow stripe still indicates that there is "no passing" through town. Mr. Yaksich and his mother lived in the second row house on the way into town from 1937 to 1944. The other houses were used as schoolrooms during that time since the original two-story school burned to the ground in 1923 and was never rebuilt. Across the street from the company houses is a larger residence on the hill that formerly served the mine's general superintendent.

A long bank of coke ovens, partially destroyed for salvage, stand along the highway and abandoned railroad right-of-way. Immediately south of them are stockpiled hills of pure coal. West of the company houses 1.7 miles stands the Koehler Coal Mine, looking very much as if it could be cranked into operation with a mere flip of a switch. Near the mine when I first visited were the town's only readily apparent residents, a large flock of wild turkeys.

The St. Louis, Rocky Mountain and Pacific Company opened the first coal mine at Koehler in 1906. The town, which was named for Henry Koehler, chairman of the Board of Directors of the Maxwell Land Grant, had a peak population of approximately eighteen hundred. Many buildings, residences, and businesses were owned by St. Louis, Rocky Mountain and Pacific, including the Blossburg Mercantile and a saloon. Baseball was the most popular sport, especially when played against arch-rival Van Houten, another S.R.M. & P. town, now virtually dismantled and owned by the National Rifle Association.

Koehler closed in 1924, opened again in 1936, only to close again in the mid-1950s. Kaiser Steel purchased the property in 1955 and has no immediate plans for the site.

CATSKILL AND STUBBLEFIELD CANYON

The ruins of Catskill and Stubblefield Canyon are behind locked gates about 32 miles northwest of Raton off York Canyon Road.

To the connoisseur, it would be the difference between a hand-tooled hunting knife and the one next to your spoon in a restaurant: in Colfax County, there are ovens and then there are *ovens.* The long lines of coke ovens at Gardiner, Dawson, and Koehler, although impressive, are no match for the charcoal ovens at Catskill and Stubblefield Canyon. Their closest competitors are at Cochran, Arizona, where five ovens stand watch over the Gila River. But here, along the Canadian River, there are two groups, one of ten and the other of fourteen.

Catskill was a thriving lumber town from 1890 to 1902, and although that certainly is a short existence, what Catskill lacked in longevity it made up for with exuberance. At its peak the town of about twenty-five hundred had four hotels; a railroad spur from Trinidad, Colorado; a school; a church for all faiths; and a ball park, picnic ground, and race course. The town became famous in northern New Mexico and southern Colorado as a place for a good-time summer weekend. The timber gave out and the railroad tracks came up in 1902. Catskill held on for a short

Catskill—rear view of ovens. Wood was loaded in this side and charcoal removed through front door after a kind of pressure cooking.

while as a cattle town, but the great weekends were over. The post office closed in 1905, and the town was abandoned.

Cattle still roam along the banks of the Canadian River, but the ranchers are leasing from Kaiser Steel. The roads into the townsite and ovens are closed by a locked gate. I was given permission by Kaiser to photograph, but the road into the townsite was extremely rough because of summer rains—impassable even to four-wheel-drive vehicles. All that remains there, according to workers who know the site well, is one corner of the old vault that was located in the general store. I drove instead into nearby Stubblefield Canyon to photograph ovens that were used to convert wood to charcoal. There, three miles north of the locked gate, were fourteen "beehive" ovens, almost 30 feet high and 30 feet in diameter and in a remarkable state of preservation, thanks to their remoteness and to the watchful eye of many over the years.

One of the great frustrations of ghost town buffs who care is the thoughtless destruction of valuable historic sites by others and the knowledge that far too few of the guilty are caught or punished. To those of you who have felt that frustration, read on. After visiting these beautifully crafted, symmetrical ovens I called Mr. Nick Yaksich at the York Canyon Mine to express my appreciation for letting me in (see Acknowledgments, page viii). He asked me if I had noticed anything unusual about one of the ovens, and I said yes, that one had brick of a slightly lighter color and that it had some rubble in front of it. It seems that a person was found destroying an oven, and he was made to rebuild it, brick by brick by brick. I only wish I could have been there to watch.

BRILLIANT CANYON: GARDINER, BLOSSBURG, SWASTIKA, AND BRILLIANT

Take South Fifth Street out of Raton and around the golf course to the locked gate. Gardiner and its coke ovens are visible from there. North 2.2 miles is Blossburg, with Swastika 0.8 miles beyond Blossburg. Brilliant is 0.5 miles north of Swastika. All sites are owned by Kaiser Steel and are private.

The first locomotive to enter New Mexico arrived in Raton, then called Willow Springs, in December 1878. Only three years later, a Santa Fe Railroad geologist, James T. Gardiner, found large deposits of coal only a few miles west of the main Santa Fe line through town. From then on, Raton and the communities in Dillon Canyon, more popularly known locally as Brilliant Canyon, prospered because of the close relationship between railroads and coal.

The first mining community was Blossburg, opened in 1881 by both the Raton Coal and Coking Company and the Santa Fe Railroad. The population peaked at about one thousand, but there was no town doctor. As a result, the first telephone in Colfax County connected Blossburg's Smith's Store to the Raton office of Dr. James Shuler.

The critical year for Blossburg was 1894. An explosion in the town's mine killed five men and injured three others, and a few months later a strike closed the mine. Never again did Blossburg enjoy full production and prosperity. Only one hundred persons lived there by 1903—and only twenty by 1939. The post office, which had opened in 1881, closed for good in 1905.

The town of Gardiner was the second one established in Dillon Canyon. In 1896 a battery of three hundred ovens was constructed there to convert coal to coke, a material used in the smelting of copper. The ovens ran in four parallel rows of one-quarter mile each and were manned

Remains of Blossburg

Ruins of power plant near Gardiner

Gardiner—residence of Tom Hay

principally by Italians, who were supposed to be able to tolerate the heat of the ovens better than others.

Gardiner, a St. Louis, Rocky Mountain and Pacific Company town with a peak population of about one thousand, lasted longer than the others; its post office closed in 1940 after forty-three years of service, but the town had a whisper of life until 1954.

At the same time Blossburg was fading in 1905, the new site of Brilliant was coming to life. Like Gardiner, Brilliant was a St. Louis, Rocky Mountain and Pacific Company town, with mines providing coal for the Santa Fe locomotives and for the Gardiner coke ovens. The population in 1907 was 350; at this time the town had such amenities as two hotels, saloons, a recreation hall, electric power, and telephones.

Swastika became a sister community to Brilliant in 1919, the year the Swastika Fuel Company (owned and operated by the St. Louis, Rocky Mountain and Pacific Company) began working coal deposits south of Brilliant. A post office opened the same year, and eventually the town could claim five hundred residents.

The post office at Brilliant closed in 1935, the same year the town died. By then Swastika had become the principal coal-producing town in Dillon Canyon. The rise of Hitler and the Nazi Party changed forever the world's perception of the swastika, an ancient design common to cultures all over the world. The town and the fuel company became, through no fault of their own, the bearers of a name fast becoming an anathema. An easy solution lay in the ghost town to the north. The post office at Swastika became Brilliant in 1940 and remained open until 1954, the year everything closed up in Brilliant Canyon. The swastika symbol was not so easily eradicated, however: it still adorns the International State Bank Building in downtown Raton.

Gardiner is the only ghost town in the canyon that a visitor can see from public property. It is also the best town of the four. One of the banks of ruined coke ovens is the most obvious remnant. At the townsite itself is a tall, narrow building that once housed a portable AC/DC power converter for the mines. A few foundations, a part of the miners' amusement hall, and two company houses remain. In one of those houses, formerly the town doctor's, lives Tom Hay, who came to Dillon Canyon in 1921 with his family. His father was a cable splicer with the mines. The Hays were the last people to live in Brilliant, and now Mr. Hay can claim the same distinction for Gardiner. Actually, he is only a part-time resident since he owns another house in Raton.

North of the coke ovens are the foundations of the coal washer and the power substation. At Blossburg, behind a second locked gate and a "no trespassing" sign, are three ruined buildings, one of them two-story, and a few structures of a working ranch.

Swastika (New Brilliant) contains foundations for about a quarter of a mile, including those up a side canyon to the north, but no buildings stand. The same is true at Brilliant.

For one weekend in the summer of 1980, New Brilliant and Brilliant Canyon exploded happily back to life. Former Brilliant resident Mrs. Loretta Moore had the wonderful idea of putting on a Brilliant reunion. She and Zita Yaksich, who also once lived in Brilliant, began a search for names and addresses of those who had left the Raton area. Their efforts proved tremendously successful since over eight hundred people came for a picnic at the site of New Brilliant on July 27, 1980. Kaiser Steel had purchased the canyon after the demise of the towns there, but the company gave great assistance to the reunion planners. I hitched a ride with a Kaiser Steel driver as he ferried portable toilets, tables, and supplies up to the reunion site. In Raton a theater marquee read "Welcome Brilliant Canyon Reunion," and talk in the town bakery was of nothing else. A gentleman I met in the delightful Tinnie's Palace restaurant had come with his wife from Colorado for the occasion, and they were thrilled at the prospect of reestablishing friendships interrupted by almost thirty years. People tend to think of corporations like Kaiser Steel as impersonal, but the people at the Brilliant Canyon Reunion and the residents of Raton will set them straight.

SUGARITE AND YANKEE

Drive east from Raton on New Mexico 72, which crosses I-25 east of town. East of that crossing 3.7 miles is a junction. Sugarite is 1.7 miles to the left; Yankee is 1.3 miles to the right.

Sugarite and Yankee, like the ghosts in Dillon Canyon, were coal towns. And, like Blossburg, Brilliant, and Swastika, there isn't too much left to see at the townsites.

Yankee became an active coal town in 1904 and eventually claimed two thousand residents. The town was named in honor of the Bostonians who provided much of the capital used to establish the community. Mines were active until the 1920s, but today the only visible traces of mining activity can be seen along the canyon walls northeast of Yankee, where several scars remain. Yankee is now a ranching and farming area.

Sugarite's cattle ranching predated its coal-mining days, which began in 1909. The town's name is a corruption of a similar-sounding word *chicorica* (also spelled "*chicarica*" or "*chicorico*"), which is still the name of the creek that runs through the canyon. Whether that name is a corruption from Spanish or Comanche is uncertain. See an interesting explanation in T. M. Pearce's *New Mexico Place Names*. Although it was a smaller community than Yankee, Sugarite outlasted its neighbor by twenty years; the last mines closed in 1941, laying off over fifty men. The only remains today are foundations on the east side of Sugarite Canyon. Heavy vegetation could be hiding many additional foundations that are not readily distinguishable.

But there is definitely something to see. South of Sugarite 0.7 miles, clearly visible on a knoll to the east, is the dramatic ruin of a mansion built by Yankee entrepreneur A. D. Ensign after the turn of the century. The mansion is in remarkable shape, considering that it has been abandoned since 1923. It certainly has been ransacked and brutalized, but the visitor can still picture the splendor of the home. Matching fireplaces face each other in the largest room. Six other fireplaces, four of them upstairs, attest to the raw winters. In 1912, for example, Yankee was so thoroughly snowbound that a train from Raton to Yankee, a distance of nine miles, took two days. A long stone stairway leads down from the house to a dramatic entrance near the orchards to the south. The Ensign mansion is one of my favorite buildings in all of New Mexico.

Ensign Mansion, abandoned since the '20s

Central business district of Folsom

BELL (JOHNSON MESA)

Bell is 11 miles southeast of Yankee and 16 miles east of Raton on New Mexico 72.

Mining ghost towns usually show considerable evidence of their former activity with dumps, adits, and foundations. Farming ghost towns can be vastly different. It is really difficult to imagine that Bell, a community of about a dozen deserted farm buildings, a cemetery, and a church, once had five schools for the children of the families on Johnson Mesa.

Johnson Mesa is a truly unusual place. As you drive along the twisting highway through the coal-bearing canyons east of Yankee, the road suddenly turns up onto an enormous plain of almost one hundred square miles, a plain that would resemble the Midwest if it weren't at eight thousand feet. Even the main roads, as is so often the case in farming states, are laid out following topographic sections. Lige Johnson, for whom the area was named, grazed his cattle on this mesa, and it was also here that railroad workers and miners, trying to find a safer and more predictable occupation, began successful farms in the 1880s. Some miners tried to juggle both occupations, so carrier pigeons dispatched from Blossburg would fly up to the mesa to notify the miners that they were needed down in the Raton Valley. The town on the mesa was Bell, named for Marion Bell, the leader of the railroaders and miners. Severe winters, the 1918 flu epidemic, difficult farming conditions, and better opportunities elsewhere led to a general exodus from the mesa, and Bell closed its post office in 1933.

Two buildings are of particular interest. St. John's Methodist Episcopal, built in 1899, is an austere but nevertheless charming church. It contains a small wooden pulpit, a guest register, a simple wooden cross, and a very warm feeling. The other building I liked is an abandoned farmhouse 1.8 miles east of the church.

FOLSOM

Folsom is 39 miles east of Raton and 19 miles east of Bell on New Mexico 72.

The Colorado and Southern Railroad cut across the northeast corner of New Mexico in the late 1880s and helped to create the town of Folsom. The area is important to archaeologists because of the "Folsom Man," whose habits were deduced

Former general merchandise, now a museum in Folsom

by artifacts such as stone weapons. The evidence is significant since it established the presence of humans in the area much earlier than previously had been believed.

Folsom is now a pleasant ranching community six miles east of the Colfax County line in Union County. It is only a partial ghost town, but it has several attractions. In town are the old railroad station, moved from the right-of-way around 1970 and now a private residence; the abandoned stone two-story Folsom Hotel; the false-front stores on the south side of the main street; and the general merchandise store, dating from 1896, now a museum. North of town are several deserted residences, St. Joseph's Church, and a cemetery east of the church. The Folsom Cemetery, south of town, features a granite memorial with a plaque to Sarah J. Rooke, who in 1908 stayed by her switchboard phoning residents to warn of a dangerous flash flood. Seventeen people died, Sarah Rooke among them, but her heroism was credited with saving many lives. The monument was erected by her fellow workers.

CAPSULE SUMMARY

MAJOR SITES

Koehler—many remains, but behind a locked gate

Dawson—only the cemetery is public, but it is unforgettable

SECONDARY SITES

Catskill—remarkable ovens, but closed to the public

Elizabethtown—a few remains with a good cemetery in a magnificent setting

Baldy Town—cabins and foundations in a beautiful, but private, location

Folsom—good buildings in a living town

Colfax—school and remnants

Gardiner—ovens, buildings, and foundations—private property

Cimarron—four or five fine structures in an active town

Rayado—three buildings of interest

MINOR SITES

Yankee—one terrific mansion

Bell—church, cemetery, and farm buildings

Blossburg—a few ruins, private

Swastika—foundations, private

Brilliant—foundations, private

Sugarite—foundations largely hidden in brush

ROAD CONDITIONS

Catskill—muddy, rough truck road (private)

Baldy Town—very rough, rocky truck road

Brilliant Canyon—good dirt road (private)

All other sites—paved roads

TRIP SUGGESTIONS

TRIP 1: Elizabethtown, Cimarron, Colfax, Dawson (cemetery), and Gardiner (Gardiner viewed from a distance)

If you are driving from Taos to Raton, these are the sites you could visit for maximum enjoyment and minimum extra driving. Add only 25 miles and about 2½ hours to the normal 105-mile journey.

TRIP 1A: Add Rayado to Trip 1

Including Rayado means 22 additional miles for

three historic buildings and a view of the extensive holdings of the Boy Scouts of America at Philmont.

TRIP 2: Sugarite, Yankee, Bell, and Folsom

Allow for 4 hours and about 75 miles round trip from Raton. While you are in Folsom, be sure to visit nearby Capulin National Monument and its dramatic volcano. You can avoid backtracking by continuing to the town of Capulin and returning to Raton via U.S. 64 and 87.

TRIP 3: Combine Trip 2, with a visit to Gardiner, to trips from Chapter Two.

Since Raton and Las Vegas both are adjacent to I-25, you can visit a number of ghost towns on a route from Santa Fe to Colorado. See p. 28 for suggestions.

Note: The following towns are private and not included in the trip suggestions: Baldy Town, Koehler, Catskill, Blossburg, Swastika, and Brilliant.

TOPOGRAPHIC MAP INFORMATION FOR CHAPTER FOUR

COLFAX COUNTY: TOWNS OF THE HIGH COUNTRY

(For map reading assistance, consult Appendix A, page 169)

Town	Topo Map Name	Size	Year	Importance*
Elizabethtown	Eagle Nest	7½′	1963	3
Baldy Town	Ute Park	15′	1955	2
Cimarron	Cimarron	15′	1955	3
Rayado	Miami	15′	1956	3
Colfax	Colfax	7½′	1971	3
Dawson	Cimarron	15′	1955	2
Koehler	Koehler	7½′	1971	2
	Saltpeter Mt.	7½′	1971	2
Catskill and Stubblefield Canyon	Casa Grande (NM-Col)	15′	1962	1
Gardiner	Raton	7½′	1971	3
Blossburg	Raton	7½′	1971	2
Swastika	Raton	7½′	1971	2
Brilliant	Tin Pan Canyon	7½′	1971	2
Sugarite	Raton	7½′	1971	3
Yankee	Yankee	7½′	1971	3
Bell	Dale Mt. (NM-Col)	7½′	1971	3
Folsom	Folsom	7½′	1972	3

*1—essential to find and/or enjoy site to the fullest
2—helpful but not essential
3—unnecessary for finding and enjoying site

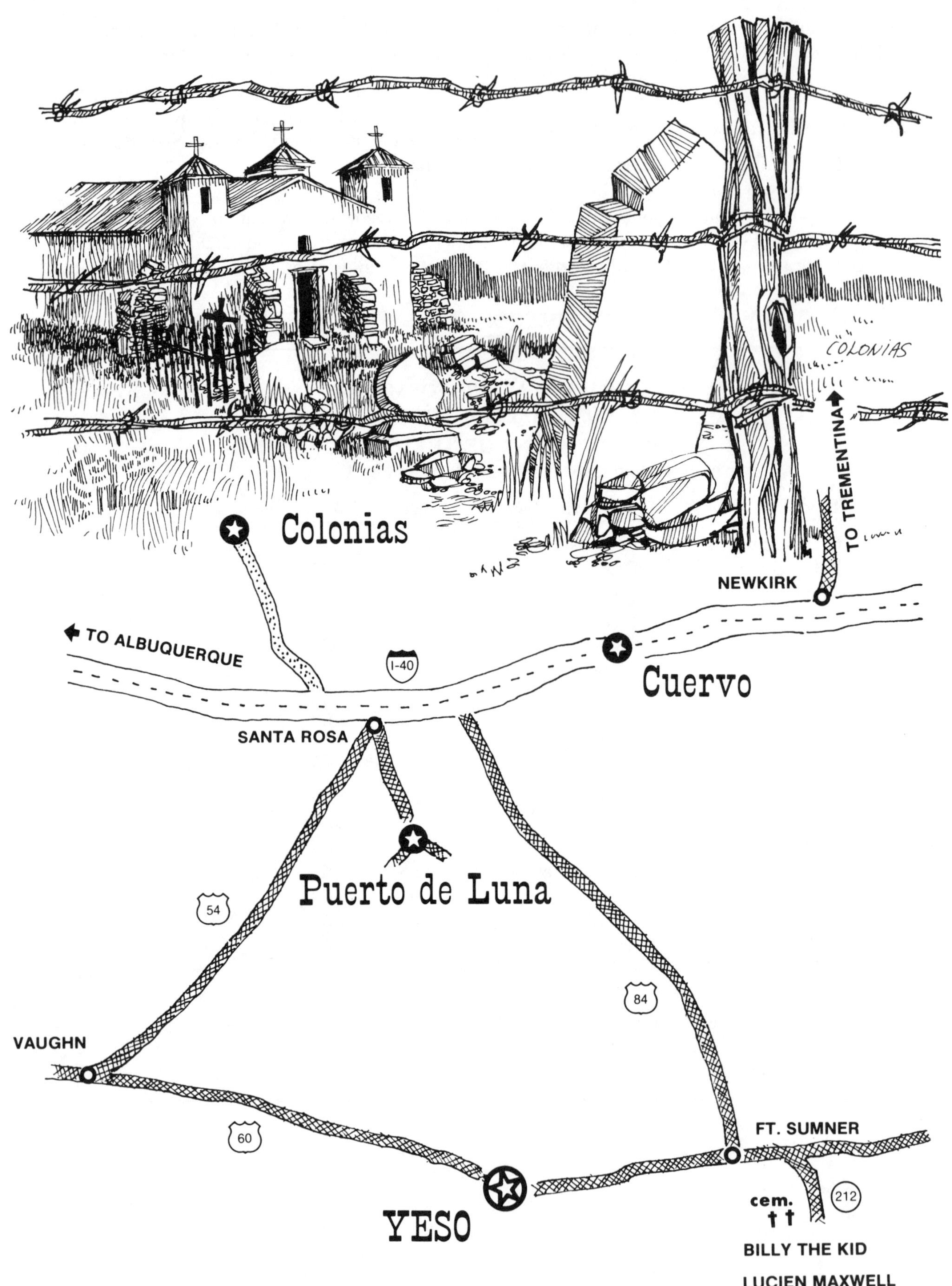
COLONIAS
TO TREMENTINA
Colonias
NEWKIRK
TO ALBUQUERQUE
I-40
Cuervo
SANTA ROSA
Puerto de Luna
54
84
VAUGHN
60
FT. SUMNER
YESO
cem.
212
BILLY THE KID
LUCIEN MAXWELL

CHAPTER FIVE

SANTA ROSA GHOSTS

THE GHOST TOWNS near Santa Rosa, 120 miles east of Albuquerque on I-40, have an intriguing variety: Colonias is a community blessed with solitude and beauty; Puerto de Luna was a bustling county seat eventually overtaken by the railroad town of Santa Rosa, a newcomer on the block; Cuervo thrived with railroads and Route 66, only to be ignored by I-40; and Yeso is split by a major highway, but it died anyway when diesels replaced locomotives.

YESO

Yeso is twenty miles west of Fort Sumner and 35 miles east of Vaughn on U.S. 60.

Yeso Creek gave this small ranching and railroad town its name, but the choice was somewhat of a misnomer. Yeso means gypsum in Spanish and refers to the unpalatable water of the creek. The town of Yeso prospered, however, because its water, pumped from nearby wells, kept cattle alive and the Santa Fe locomotives running. When diesels made the water stop obsolete, the town began to die. The school, W.P.A.-built in 1940, closed around 1966. According to a current resident, everyone except four families eventually moved to nearby Fort Sumner.

Yeso is a terrific ghost town. The two-story hotel is still pretty much intact. The Super Service Drive In and Antique Shop is a photogenic shell. The main street features a post office (still open) that contains dozens of bottles. Off the main street are several deserted homes and the school, now a private residence. Nearby is an assortment of automobiles, including a very restorable Packard. On the east end of town is a complex that once apparently included a gas station, garage, and residence or motel that proclaims—in bottlecaps set in cement—that it was established June 8, 1929.

COLONIAS

Take I-40 west from Santa Rosa to the Colonias turnoff. Colonias is 11 miles north on a fairly good dirt road.

It doesn't seem possible that the road to this picturesque, high desert community of about two dozen buildings begins at an interstate exit with a Stuckey's. A pecan shoppe and Colonias just aren't compatible.

Colonias is a ranching town on the Pecos that may have been named because a kind of "colony" was formed by employees of various ranches to work the area. Today the community features all sorts of discarded farm implements, wagons, and a corral near the center of town. The school up on the hill is now a private residence, but several interesting deserted adobe and rock masonry buildings are nearby. The unusual three-steeple

Yeso: abandoned residence

Combination gas station, garage, motel in Yeso

Service is no longer super at Yeso's drive-in

Cut stone residence in Colonias

San Jose Church at Colonias

Former county courthouse in Puerto de Luna

Cut sandstone grave markers in the cemetery at Colonias

San Jose Catholic Church, surrounded by a cemetery that has many beautifully handcrafted sandstone gravestones, is the prominent building of the town. Indeed, the church seems a foundation of the society, as a cross stands on a nearby bluff and many homes feature images and candles. The town, like nearby Puerto de Luna, has a distinctly nineteenth-century look about it. Standing on the main street, *I* felt like the anachronism, not Colonias, until my solitude was shattered by two jets that careened across the town at a disturbingly low altitude. I would have preferred a horse-drawn wagon.

PUERTO DE LUNA

Puerto de Luna is 10 miles south of Santa Rosa on New Mexico 91.

The Historical Atlas of New Mexico, by Warren A. Beck and Ynez D. Haase, shows a map of New Mexico's principal towns and railroads in 1890, eleven years after the coming of the first railroad. Puerto de Luna was the only town in the southeastern quarter of the entire state with a population of over five hundred people. Forty years later, there were eighteen towns in the same area with a population of over one thousand. And Puerto de Luna was not one of them. As the railroad and the automobile changed the makeup of the state, Puerto de Luna remained a small ranching and farming community.

Dr. Pearce states in *New Mexico Place Names* that there is disagreement about the meaning of the town's name. It is either "Luna's Gap," named for the Luna family that settled there, or (more romantically) "Gateway of the Moon," because of a gap in the mountains through which the moon sometimes shines.

Settled in 1863, Puerto de Luna once held the county seat, but the seat was moved after the turn of the century to nearby Santa Rosa, a Southern Pacific railroad town that did change with the times. Today the stone county courthouse stands abandoned in a field a short distance from the center of Puerto de Luna. Dominating the town is the unusual Nuestra Señora de Refugio Catholic Church, built in 1882 and remodeled with a rock facade in 1921. Across from the post office is another building worth investigating, a store and saloon frequented by Billy the Kid. Perhaps it is the same 1860s saloon in which Billy was reported to have killed a man in a Puerto de Luna brawl.

CUERVO

Cuervo is located 17 miles east of Santa Rosa on I-40.

Settled originally when the Southern Pacific came through the area between 1901 and 1903, Cuervo, apparently named for the crows in the vicinity, enjoyed additional prosperity around 1910 when a land boom opened the area to cattle and later sheep ranching. Route 66, now a mere frontage road on the north side of Interstate 40, created a supplemental trade of gas stations and hotels.

At its peak, Cuervo featured two schools, two hotels, two doctors, and two churches. Today, only one of those schools and the two churches remain, along with a number of other buildings. The attractive Catholic church, which was constructed during World War I, stands on the south side of I-40 along with most of the town's residences, many of which are still occupied. Of particular interest in the neighborhood is a house built of railroad ties. Also on the south side of the interstate is the one remaining school, built around 1930 and closed in 1958. Along the railroad tracks is the largest, most substantial build-

Puerto de Luna's Nuestra Señora de Refugio Catholic Church

Catholic church in Cuervo

ing in town, a warehouse with a tin roof.

Cuervo was literally buried by I-40, which cut a swath through the residential section and made the town that once depended upon the cross-country traveler into an off-ramp curiosity.

Right: Cuervo public school

CAPSULE SUMMARY

MAJOR SITE

Yeso—over a dozen structures to look at, walk around, and photograph

SECONDARY SITES

Colonias—unusual church and cemetery, several abandoned buildings

Puerto de Luna—the courthouse and church are principal attractions

Cuervo—several buildings on either side of I-40

ROAD CONDITIONS

Colonias—good dirt road for passenger cars (except in bad weather)

All other sites—paved roads

TRIP SUGGESTIONS

TRIP 1: Colonias, Puerto de Luna, and Cuervo

If you want to stay close to the interstate going to and/or from Albuquerque or Las Vegas, see these three. Round trip from Albuquerque, 320 miles. Plan for 8–10 hours.

TRIP 1A: Add Trementina to Trip 1

See Trip 3, p. 29 in Chapter Two. Leave early, arrive late from Albuquerque.

TRIP 1B: Add Yeso and Fort Sumner to Trip 1

While visiting Yeso, don't overlook Fort Sumner and the graves of Lucien Maxwell and William Bonney. Round trip distance from Albuquerque (returning through Vaughn, Encino, and Clines Corners), 400 miles. Make this an overnight.

TRIP 2: Combine Yeso and Fort Sumner with Trip 1a, p. 95 in Chapter Seven.

TOPOGRAPHIC MAP INFORMATION FOR CHAPTER FIVE

SANTA ROSA GHOSTS

(For map reading assistance, consult Appendix A, page 169)

Town	Topo Map Name	Size	Year	Importance*
Yeso	Yeso	7½′	1966	3
Colonias	Colonias	7½′	1963	3
Puerto de Luna	Puerto de Luna	7½′	1963	3
Cuervo	Cuervo	7½′	1963	3

*1—essential to find and/or enjoy site to the fullest
2—helpful but not essential
3—unnecessary for finding and enjoying site

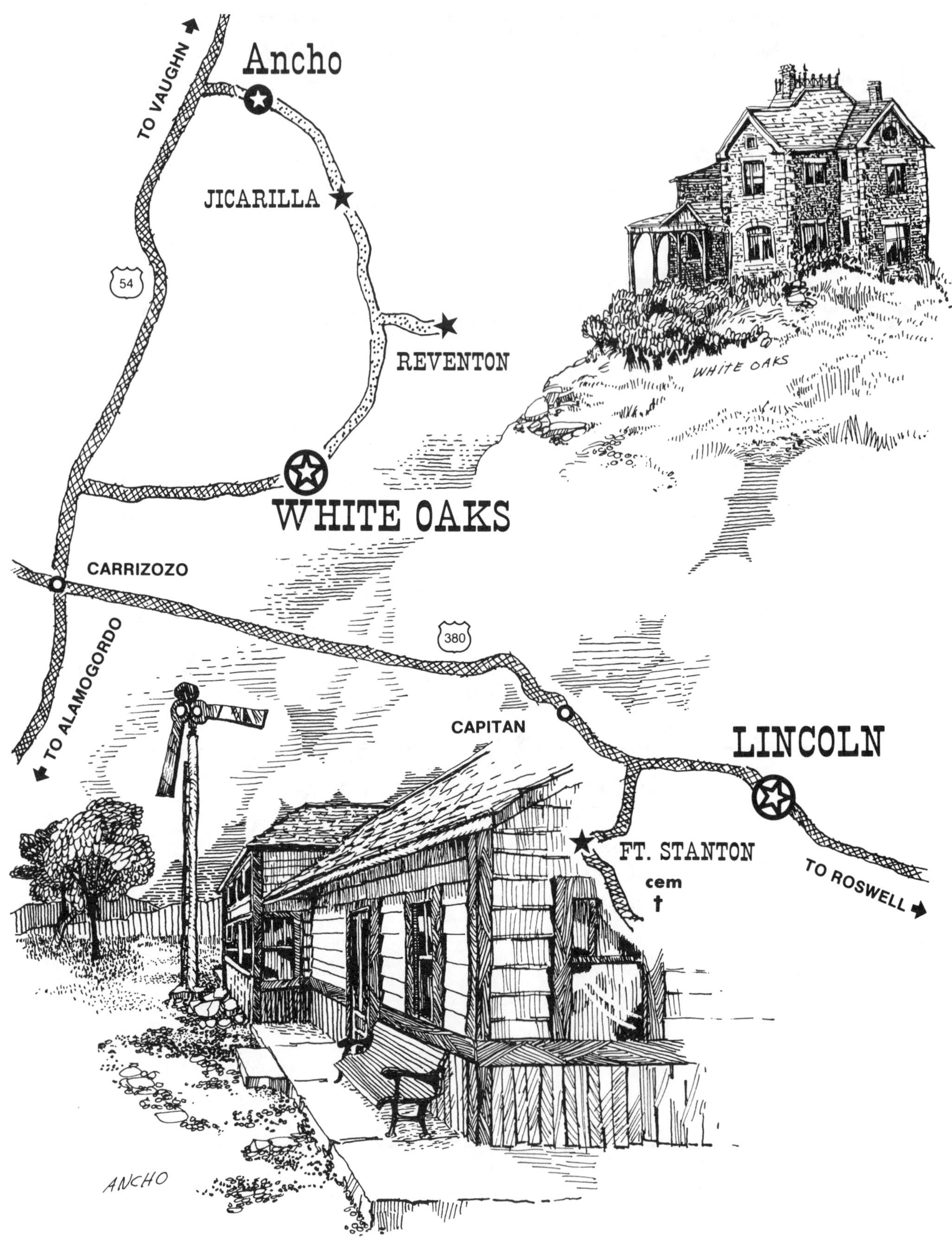

Ancho
TO VAUGHN
JICARILLA
54
REVENTON
WHITE OAKS
WHITE OAKS
CARRIZOZO
380
TO ALAMOGORDO
CAPITAN
LINCOLN
FT. STANTON
cem
TO ROSWELL
ANCHO

CHAPTER SIX

LINCOLN COUNTY: THE WAR AND THE KID

THIS IS BILLY THE KID COUNTRY, the stuff of western legend. That a young punk should be remembered above all the real men of the area is an injustice, so perhaps we should call it McSween, Tunstall, and Chisum Country. Unfortunately, legend and misrepresented romance will no doubt prevail, and visitors from all over the world will troop to Lincoln to see where Billy made his daring escape. One can only hope that they will stick around long enough to learn the names of the real heroes.

LINCOLN

Lincoln is 32 miles southeast of Carrizozo on U.S. 380.

Now more accurately an historic town rather than a ghost town, Lincoln is the scene of a time frozen in legend; the Lincoln County War and the names of Pat Garrett, Billy the Kid, and John Chisum are as embedded in western lore as Tombstone's gunfight at the O.K. Corral. But unlike Tombstone, Lincoln is a town of subtle shades of history. It is quite possible, for example, for a tourist to whisk through town and never know what happened there, which certainly is preferable to being bombarded by garish signs while modern buildings intrude upon the ambience of the place. Civic leaders in "ghost towns" like Colorado's Central City, Arizona's Tombstone, and Nevada's Virginia City could benefit from a visit to Lincoln. Dozens of buildings line the highway through town. Many of them are fully restored, some by individual owners, and more are in the process of restoration funded by a group of concerned preservationists. Only once a year, for "Billy the Kid Days," does Lincoln explode into the flagrant tourist business so prevalent in other famous towns; but afterwards it returns to its quiet self, and one can almost hear the collective sigh from the residents as the hordes depart, for then the dedicated task of restoration can begin once more.

Originally, Lincoln was La Placita del Rio Bonito, settled by Spaniards in 1849. They were harassed often enough by Mescalero Apaches that they needed a kind of fortress, the Torreon, for refuge. It still stands. In 1869, when a new county was created and named for the assassinated president, La Placita's name was changed to Lincoln, and it was designated the county seat.

The conflict behind the Lincoln County War of 1878 began in 1873, when L. G. Murphy, James J. Dolan, and Emil Fritz were removed as the business agents in nearby Fort Stanton because of alleged improprieties with both the military and Indian accounts. The company moved to Lincoln and, through powerful friends including

Tunstall's store, Lincoln

the territorial governor, procured the same kinds of Fort Stanton and Indian contracts they had lost previously at the fort.

In 1875, a high-principled, intelligent lawyer named Alexander McSween and his wife Susan moved to Lincoln, followed a year later by a young Englishman, John H. Tunstall. By April of 1877, the two men aligned themselves against the Murphy-Dolan faction and went so far as to begin construction on a store to compete with the established Murphy-Dolan one. Respected rancher John Chisum joined with McSween and Tunstall in plans for the formation of a bank. Unfortunately, Murphy and Dolan, who obviously were not amused by the competition for "their" town, had two things McSween and Tunstall did not: political power and the sheriff. McSween was arrested on a ludicrous charge of embezzlement arising from a legal matter with James Dolan, and the sheriff, one William Brady, impounded the Tunstall-McSween store to be held in judgment against the embezzlement charge. He then moved, on February 18, 1878, to secure Tunstall's ranch property, which had no economic connection with McSween. In doing so, Sheriff Brady's men murdered John Tunstall after ordering him, weaponless and surrounded, to dismount.

Eventually friends of McSween and the late Tunstall formed a group of vigilantes known as the Regulators, one of whom was Henry McCarty (also known as William Antrim, William H. Bonney, Billy Bonney, or merely the Kid). No one knew him as Billy the Kid except Pat Garrett, who called him "Billy, the Kid," according to author-historian Leon Metz. Bonney had joined Tunstall's following at the age of eighteen in 1877.

On April 1, 1878, the Regulators gained a measure of revenge by gunning down Sheriff Brady on the main street of Lincoln. Several skirmishes of the Lincoln County War followed, the final act of which began on July 14, 1878. Alex McSween, who had known ever since Tunstall's death that he was next, and who had been hiding in various locations around Lincoln County including John Chisum's ranch, rode with about fifty Regulators into Lincoln to make a final stand. Sporadic fighting took place over the next few days, and on July 19, McSween's house was set ablaze by the dep-

Lincoln—Dolan House

uties of Sheriff Peppin, Brady's successor. Susan McSween, who had been with her husband during the entire siege, begged for a truce, but it was not granted. Later in the day, during a surrender attempt in which someone fired a shot, Alexander McSween was killed.

An investigation into alleged improprieties squarely supported the Tunstall-McSween faction. The governor of the territory resigned, the colonel at Fort Stanton was relieved of his command, and Sheriff Peppin was also forced to resign. James Dolan, however, prospered: by 1882 he owned Tunstall's store and his ranch.

William Bonney lived until the summer of 1880. Sentenced to hang for the murder of Sheriff Brady, Bonney made a daring escape from the Lincoln County courthouse (formerly the Murphy-Dolan store) by murdering two deputies. It is this escape that is reenacted during Billy the Kid Days. Two months after his escape, the Kid was dead, shot in the dark by Sheriff Pat Garrett at old Fort Sumner.

You will find any number of sights to see in Lincoln. The obvious are the courthouse (the old Murphy-Dolan store), Tunstall's store, and the Dolan house. But don't overlook the Wortley Hotel (a replica of the original), the doctor's residence, the Montaño store, the Ellis and Sons Store (now a magnificent, rambling residence), and the cemetery southeast of town. But the graves of the principal characters of the Lincoln County War are not there. William Bonney, the Kid, is buried in a cemetery near old Fort Sumner, a few miles southeast of the present town. Nearby is the grave of Lucien Maxwell, land baron of New Mexico (see Cimarron and Rayado, p. 44). Susan McSween eventually remarried, became known as the Cattle Queen of New Mexico, and lived in White Oaks, where she died in 1931 (see White Oaks, p. 72). Alex McSween and John Tunstall, the two men who heroically fought corruption and power—and lost, are buried in Lincoln, but you'll have to look around a bit. Out behind the Tunstall Store, hidden in tall grass, are two simple brass markers, side by side:

Alex A. McSween	John H. Tunstall
1843–1878	1853–1878

White Oaks—the Exchange Bank Building, its block facade gone

FORT STANTON

Fort Stanton is south of the main highway on a clearly marked turnoff between Lincoln and Capitan on U.S. 380.

Since it was alleged improprieties at Fort Stanton that really provided the beginnings of the quarrels that led to the Lincoln County War, you might enjoy a short side trip to see the fort itself.

Fort Stanton, named for a captain who had been killed by Mescalero Apaches, was established in 1855 to control the activity of that same tribe. The original fort was burned and abandoned by its own troops in 1861 so that it could not be used by an approaching Confederate army. Rebuilt in 1868, the fort eventually housed two hundred men with jurisdiction over a Mescalero Apache reservation that covered 144 square miles. Abandoned by the army in 1896, the fort became a tuberculosis treatment center for U.S. Merchant Marine seamen. During World War II, German prisoners were interned there. The state of New Mexico has used the facility as a hospital since 1953.

On a road leading southeast from the main building is the cemetery filled with Merchant Marines who were, one must assume, tuberculosis victims. Across a deserted stretch of the cemetery, in a lonely corner, are the graves of four German captives who died in 1942.

WHITE OAKS

White Oaks is 11 miles from Carrizozo. Drive northeast from Carrizozo on U.S. 54 and turn right on New Mexico 349.

White Oaks might not be the somnolent ghost town it now is were it not for its former residents' own greed. In the late 1890s, both the Santa Fe and the El Paso and Northeastern railroads were planning to extend tracks toward White Oaks. Prominent businessmen in town were so certain

White Oaks—the Gumm residence

of a bidding war for the privilege of a railroad's being allowed to enter their town that they asked outrageous prices for the right-of-way. The El Paso and Northeastern took its collective tracks and went home, so to speak, and bypassed the town by ten miles. From that point on, White Oaks began to decline.

It was, however, once known as the liveliest town in the territory. The commotion began after a miner named Baxter found a gold deposit in the Jicarilla Mountains in 1879. Within a year, the town, named for the white oaks surrounding a nearby spring, was a tent community with a post office. By 1885 the town was much more substantial, and a reporter from Denver remarked that the people there were of "intelligence and culture," and that their influence ". . . had an ennobling effect on pioneer life and aided in the molding of a frontier society into more refined, cultured and virtuous channels." By the late 1880s, White Oaks's culture was reflected in its buildings, the best of which still stand. On the main street into town, White Oaks Avenue, stands the Exchange Bank Building, also known as the Hewett Building. It is, unfortunately, somewhat like a painting for which only a hand-carved frame remains, the canvas long gone, for the building's owners stripped it of its stone facade for use in a private residence. North of the bank is the two-story brick schoolhouse, which, despite its considerable size, has only four classrooms—two upstairs and two down. Beyond the school is the Gumm residence—a wooden Victorian lavishly furnished in rosewood and mahogany that was constructed by a family who owned sawmills and a woodworking factory in the area.

On a hill south of the main street stands the Hoyle mansion, a dramatic brick Victorian built in 1887 by Watson Hoyle, who made his fortune as a one-twelfth owner of the Old Abe, the most profitable gold mine near White Oaks. A story persists that Hoyle built the house for a bride

Four-room brick schoolhouse in White Oaks

who refused him and that, as a consequence, he never lived in the house; long-time resident Morris Parker, however, flatly debunked the tale and claimed that Hoyle lived in the house for years. The home cost between $40,000 and $70,000, while the town's impressive schoolhouse cost only $10,000. Two classic Victorian homes remain in White Oaks, and even though one is of brick and the other of wood, the visitor notices striking similarities between the two, and it is no wonder: the Gumms used the plans of the Hoyle house, reversed, when they built their monument to success.

If White Oaks had the "intelligence" and "culture" that the Denver reporter noted, how did it become known as the "liveliest town in the territory"? There was another side to White Oaks, and it was a section called Hogtown—where bars, casinos, dance halls, and brothels flourished. The most famous faro dealer in the casinos of White Oaks was Madame Varnish, so called because she was a "slick" dealer—no doubt many a miner was shellacked. Billy the Kid was an occasional visitor to town, but Pat Garrett was the sheriff in the early 1880s. Overall, however, Morris Parker recalled White Oaks as an essentially civilized place, with such refinements as an opera house, drama clubs, and literary societies.

On your way in to White Oaks, be sure to stop at the Cedarvale Cemetery, established in 1880 by the Knights of Pythias. Citizens important to both White Oaks and New Mexico are buried there: W. C. McDonald, once a White Oaks surveyor and later the first New Mexico governor after statehood; Susan McSween Barber (her name misspelled on her gravestone), a survivor of the Lincoln County War (see Lincoln entry, p. 69) and later known as the Cattle Queen of New Mexico; John Wilson, one of the original discoverers of the gold strike; and David "Jack" Jackson and his wife Mary, the only black residents of White Oaks. Jackson arrived in 1897 and witnessed the decline of the town from its late boom days. It was a virtual ghost town just after the

The Hoyle mansion, home of more legends and rumors than residents

turn of the century, but Jack Jackson stayed on, maintaining the graveyard voluntarily, carrying soup to sick community residents, and even oiling mining machinery in abandoned mines so that if the mines ever opened again the equipment would not be rusted. He died in 1963 and now rests in the cemetery he helped to preserve.

White Oaks may have lost the railroad, but it gained its own kind of permanence even in decline, for although the big mines are closed, the beauty of this "mountain paradise," as Morris Parker called it, remains. The buildings of White Oaks are among the most attractive and photogenic in New Mexico, and memories of people like David Jackson and Susan McSween Barber are intensified by a visit to the Cedarvale Cemetery.

REVENTON

Drive northeast out of White Oaks, taking the left fork. The first turnoff to Reventon is 5.1 miles from White Oaks. The second is 0.5 miles farther, at a gate marked "no trespassing."

Reventon (also Rabenton and Raventon) is a minor ghost town that prospered principally as a farming and ranching community during the boom days of White Oaks. The post office, granted in 1896, was for Raventon; it was reopened in 1910 as Rabenton, closing finally in 1928. The topographic map identifies the community as Reventon, along Reventon Draw. The two ranchers I spoke to said they spelled it the latter way.

Jim and Barbara Sherman's *Ghost Towns and Mining Camps of New Mexico* shows photographs of the townsite that is now closed to visitors. I did learn, however, that the vacant schoolhouse the Shermans refer to is now a private residence. The Shermans also reported a teacherage, rock ruins of an old school and of a post office, and adobe store ruins. I did gain access to another section of Reventon containing the small cemetery and the house of the Sedillo family, the original homesteaders in the area. The 1973 White

Sedillo homestead, Reventon

Log schoolhouse near Jicarilla

Combination store, post office, and assay office at the main townsite of Jicarilla

Oaks North 7½′ map shows the relative position of the town to the cemetery and house.

JICARILLA

The log schoolhouse at Jicarilla is 5.5 miles north of the northern Reventon turnoff and 11.1 miles northeast of White Oaks. The townsite is 0.7 miles north of the schoolhouse.

They've been finding placer gold off and on for 130 years at Jicarilla, and they're still busy at it today. On my first visit in 1979, a gentleman showed me some small vials containing his findings; when I returned in 1980, the operations in the area were more sophisticated, although still small time compared to some in other parts of the state.

The town was named for the mountain range the town is located in, and the range was named for the Jicarilla (Basketmaker) Apaches. Mexicans worked the placer deposits in the 1850s, and Americans began arriving for the same purpose in the 1880s. In a classic example of the U.S. government's treatment of the Apaches, the Jicarilla Indian Reservation was abolished by Congress shortly after gold was found on it. The town's post office opened in 1892. A log schoolhouse was built in 1907 and remained in use through the Depression, when hundreds of out-of-work people survived on what they could pan from the creeks.

The log schoolhouse stands today, south of town; a later schoolhouse, constructed in the 1930s, is located in town and is now a residence. A false front—the former post office, assay office, and store—stands next to an occupied home.

ANCHO

Ancho is 7.4 miles north of Jicarilla and 2.5 miles from U.S. 54 at a point 21.5 miles northeast of Carrizozo.

When the El Paso and Northeastern railway came through the Ancho (wide) Valley between 1899 and 1901, a railroad stop was established for ranching and shipping in the area. This stop grew into a small town named for the valley. The community, however, was destined for bigger things. A year later a gypsum deposit was discovered

Ancho's My House of Old Things

Center of the action in the old El Paso and Northeastern station, now My House of Old Things

nearby, and the Gypsum Product Company plaster mill was built. Then fire clay was found, resulting in the development of the town's major industry—the Ancho Brick Plant. The community continued to grow; a large railroad station was built in 1902, and company houses lined the main streets of town. Ancho plaster helped rebuild San Francisco after the 1906 earthquake, and Ancho bricks were used in the smelter stacks at Douglas, Arizona. Phelps Dodge bought the brick plant in 1917 and enlarged it, but production ceased in 1921. After lying idle for a few years, the plant was demolished for salvage in 1937.

An Ancho brick school, built in the 1930s and closed in 1955, stands on the western edge of what is left of the town. Three company homes remain, as well as a closed store and gas station. The cemetery is about 0.4 miles northeast of town. But the best reason to see Ancho is the old depot, moved from the right-of-way and turned into My House of Old Things, a wonderful conglomeration of all the things you thought nobody

Crumbling company house at Ancho

The Ancho school, built—naturally—with Ancho bricks

Ancho brick

had saved. Anything that could be considered a collectible—pencils, arrowheads, furniture, and even a baseball uniform—is there; the variety is charming. Mrs. Jackie Silvers was the force behind the project although others donated some of the items. Her daughter, Mrs. Sara Jackson, now runs My House of Old Things. I cannot call it merely a museum, for nearly every small town seems to be getting one of those, and ghost town enthusiasts should be getting wary of them. This former depot is an experience not to be overlooked.

CAPSULE SUMMARY

MAJOR SITES

White Oaks—several excellent buildings

Lincoln—historic town, not overly commercial

SECONDARY SITE

Ancho—My House of Old Things is unique.

MINOR SITES

Jicarilla—good log schoolhouse

Fort Stanton—now a state hospital

Reventon—private property

ROAD CONDITIONS

Jicarilla—good passenger car dirt road

Reventon—dirt road, private property

All other sites—paved roads

TRIP SUGGESTIONS

Carrizozo, 145 miles from both El Paso, Texas, and Albuquerque, New Mexico, is the central town of size in the area and has the most accommodations. Excellent meals and lodgings, however, are available at several other communities, notably Lincoln, Tinnie, and Ruidoso.

TRIP 1: Lincoln, Fort Stanton, White Oaks, Jicarilla, Ancho

Go to Lincoln first because that's where the fame of the region really originates. Backtrack to White Oaks and take the pleasant loop up to Ancho. Plan to spend all day in the area; an overnight would be ideal. Round trip from Carrizozo, 110 miles.

TRIP 1A: Add Fort Sumner and Puerto de Luna to Trip 1 (see Chapter Five, p. 61)

If you want to trace the adventures of Billy the Kid further, see his grave at Fort Sumner and

one of his haunts at Puerto de Luna. Of course, if you want to see all the spots he is supposed to have toured, you'll need to crisscross New Mexico; see the index for quick reference.

TRIP 1B: Combine Trip 1 with towns in Chapter Seven (see p. 83)

Carrizozo is only 64 miles from San Antonio and the towns in that area.

TRIP 2: Lincoln, White Oaks, and Ancho

If you want to see the best towns and don't want to leave the pavement, you can ignore Jicarilla and drive from White Oaks up to Ancho. Round trip from Carrizozo, about 120 miles.

TOPOGRAPHIC MAP INFORMATION FOR CHAPTER SIX

LINCOLN COUNTY: THE WAR AND THE KID

(For map reading assistance, consult Appendix A, page 169)

Town	Topo Map Name	Size	Year	Importance*
Lincoln	Lincoln	15′	1961	3
Fort Stanton	Fort Stanton	7½′	1963	3
White Oaks	White Oaks North	7½′	1973	3
	White Oaks South	7½′	1973	3
Reventon	White Oaks North	7½′	1973	1
Jicarilla	White Oaks North	7½′	1973	3
Ancho	Ancho	7½′	1973	3

*1—essential to find and/or enjoy site to the fullest
2—helpful but not essential
3—unnecessary for finding and enjoying site

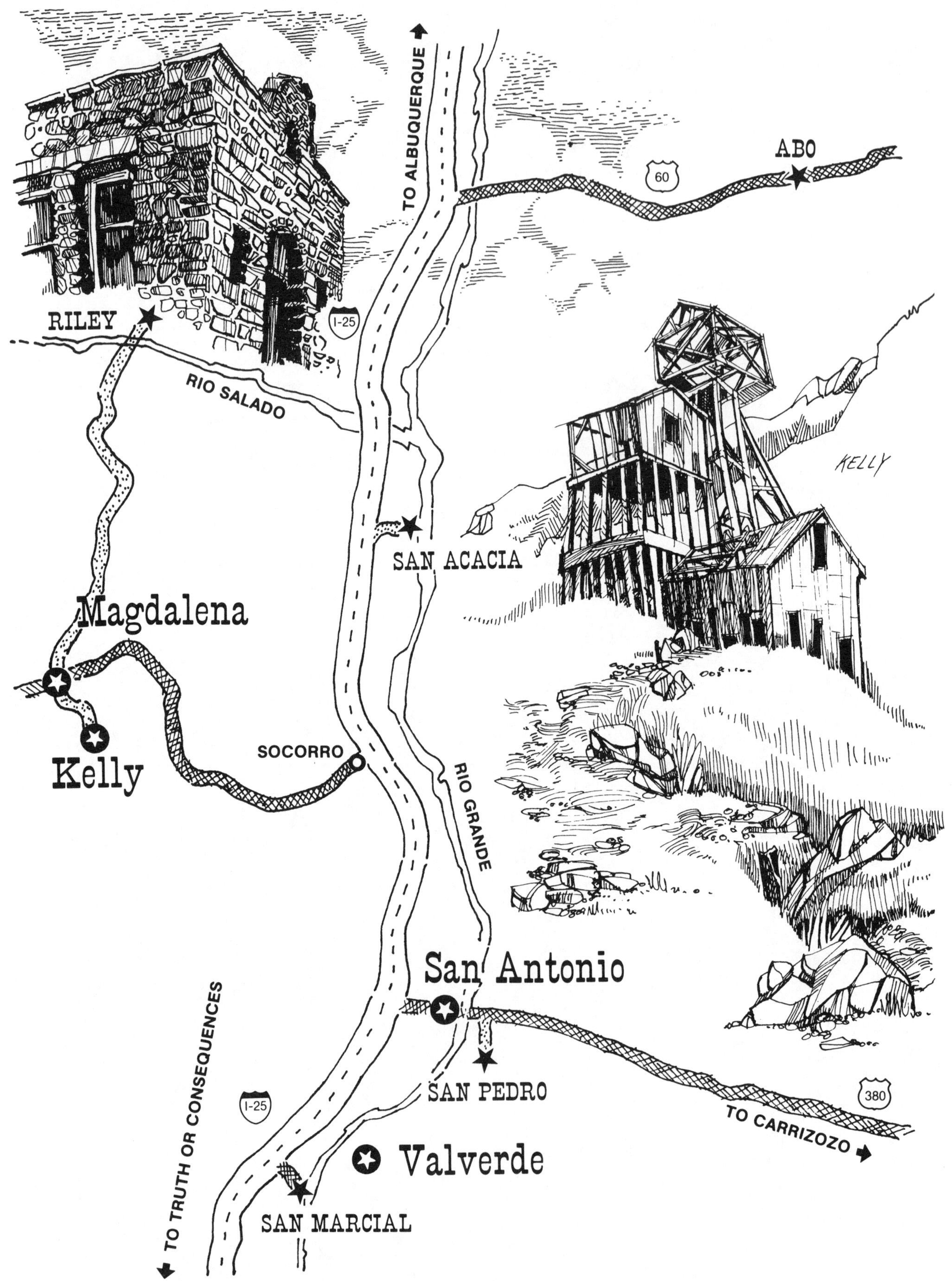

TO ALBUQUERQUE
ABO
60
RILEY
I-25
RIO SALADO
KELLY
SAN ACACIA
Magdalena
Kelly
SOCORRO
RIO GRANDE
San Antonio
TO TRUTH OR CONSEQUENCES
SAN PEDRO
I-25
380
TO CARRIZOZO
Valverde
SAN MARCIAL

CHAPTER SEVEN

GHOSTS OF THE RIO GRANDE

SOCORRO, seventy-five miles south of Albuquerque on I-25, is one of New Mexico's freeway towns that tourists usually see only the worst of—the strung-out, travel-trade fast-food restaurants and gas stations. Like so many other New Mexico towns, those rows of businesses arrived late; Socorro's historic center is where the community's quiet beauty can best be seen. Come in the morning as patrons eat sweets at the outdoor tables of the Mexican bakery and the old-timers stake out their spots on the plaza.

Socorro is the center for visiting all the ghosts of the Rio Grande. South towards San Marcial are the old farming towns along Jornada Del Muerto, "journey of death," the caravan route between Chihuahua and Santa Fe. West of Socorro are the mining towns near the Magdalena Mountains. To the north are the small sites of San Acacia and Abo, and to the east some seventy-five miles are the ghosts of Lincoln County (see Chapter Six, p. 69).

SAN ACACIA

San Acacia is 0.5 miles east of I-25 at a point 14 miles north of Socorro.

San Acacia is a small, quiet community bordering the Santa Fe Railroad and the canals that have changed the course of the Rio Grande. It was named for San Acacio, a Roman soldier who was martyred for his Christian beliefs. According to T. M. Pearce, the last letter in the name might have been altered because of confusion with the acacia tree.

Today a few occupied buildings, a vacant school, and a small church overgrown with brush comprise the town. Northeast of San Acacia, along the canal bank, is a small cemetery.

The hill east of the cemetery is important to cartographers and ghost town enthusiasts because it was on that hill, in 1855, that John W. Garretson fixed the Initial Point for the Principal Meridian and the Base Line, a point from which all topographic maps in the state are plotted. Interestingly enough, the San Acacia topographic map (which includes the site) does not show that intersection. It must be inferred from drawing lines extending from the Range and Township lines provided. Those lines pass through the benchmark that indicates the spot.

SAN ANTONIO

San Antonio is 11 miles south of Socorro just off I-25 on U.S. 380.

San Antonio is a community that has literally changed with the times, having moved twice from its first location. The site was originally a mission founded in 1629. Eventually a small settlement grew up near the church. When the

San Acacia School

San Antonio—Crystal Palace

Santa Fe station, now off the right-of-way

Santa Fe Railroad came through and sent a branch line off to the Carthage-Tokay coal mines, the town moved south a bit and clustered around the station. The tracks were torn up in the 1890s. Today the town's gravity has shifted toward U.S. 380 and I-25—with a post office, gas station, grocery store, and a bar-restaurant as the main buildings.

The buildings of the middle era are the ones ghost town enthusiasts will seek. South of present-day San Antonio 0.7 miles are approximately ten buildings and foundations, including the Crystal Palace with its excellent false front, the old post office (the storefront building with the peaked roof), and the San Antonio railroad station, standing on blocks off of the right-of-way.

The post office faces a mere trace of a foundation that contains the makings of an American legend. It was at this location that A. H. Hilton, who came to San Antonio in the 1880s, opened a successful mercantile store, bank, and hotel. On Christmas Day, 1887, his son Conrad was born. Thirty-two years later Conrad Hilton, who started in San Antonio as a baggage carrier for his father's guests, bought his first hotel.

A fire destroyed the A. H. Hilton Mercantile Store in the early 1940s, but the beautifully crafted wooden bar was saved and installed in the Owl Bar and Restaurant in 1945. The bar, a "registered cultural property" of the state of New Mexico (a plaque in the Owl testifies to the fact), was made by Brunswick Balke Collender Company, which was later to become more famous for making bowling balls. Incidentally, the Owl claims to have the best hamburgers in the world. I ate them for three straight days, and I do not think it is an idle boast.

SAN PEDRO

Drive east from San Antonio on U.S. 380 for 1.4 miles and turn south. The cemetery will be on the left, and the townsite is just down the road.

San Pedro consists of over a dozen buildings including a two-room school, a long adobe residence, and an attractive adobe and wood church with steeple.

San Pedro, settled principally by the Tefoya and Montoya families, was an old Spanish agricultural community along the Rio Grande, but the riverbed is dry now because canals have altered the natural course of the water. Grapes were a specialty of the area with wine "sent all

Church in San Pedro

Cemetery at San Pedro

Large adobe ruin in San Pedro

Church ruins at Valverde

the way to Kansas," according to a resident. Eventually some of the citizens became miners, commuting to the nearby coal towns of Tokay and Carthage. A fierce baseball rivalry developed between San Pedro and Tokay, along with a third town—Bosquecito.

The schoolhouse was W.P.A.-built in 1936. Ironically, it closed shortly thereafter. The San Pedro Catholic Church is partially hidden among some trees southwest of the school. The building next to it was a barbershop. The large adobe directly north of the church was the home of a prominent landowner. Visible from U.S. 380 is the sandswept and desolate San Pedro cemetery.

VALVERDE

Valverde is about 15 miles south of San Antonio and 3.5 miles east of San Marcial. The townsite, however, is on private property. To reach it, you must get permission from the owners and make about a 65-mile round trip from San Antonio.

Valverde is enticing because relatively little has been written about it. The site is absolutely abandoned and part of the Diamond A Ranch. It is closed to visitors without permission to enter.

Valverde was named either for its surroundings, a "green valley," or for Captain Don Antonio Valverde y Cosio, acting governor from 1717 to 1722. The spot where the town is located was a crossing point on the Rio Grande for the Apaches and Navajos and was settled as early as 1820 by Spaniards. But it had been abandoned by 1846, probably because of constant Indian harassment, when Kit Carson and General Stephen W. Kearny camped there among some ruins.

In 1862 Confederate and Union troops fought near the site as the South's forces, under General Henry Sibley, moved north through the territory. The first encounter of what is now known as the Battle of Valverde was fought near Fort Craig on February 16. The major confrontation, however, was fought five days later very near the townsite and resulted in a Confederate victory. General Sibley, who had commanded troops at Fort Union prior to joining the Confederacy, was subsequently defeated a month later by troops

The cemetery at Valverde, looking southwest, with school ruin in the right background and Black Mesa on the far left

Only one wall, with the blackboard gone, remains of the school at Valverde.

from his former fort, aided by Colorado volunteers, at the Battle of Glorieta Pass.

Valverde became a small farming and ranching community after the threat of Indian attack passed. Today only a few adobe walls, many hidden by the dense brush, mark the residences of the town, but the adobe church is still quite identifiable with its tin roof and steeple. A wall, foundations, and steps of the school (closed in 1934) stand southeast of the church; a cemetery, practically buried by shifting sands, is northeast of the school. A rancher who was born in neighboring San Marcial in 1911 told me that about fifty families used to live in the immediate area and sent their children to the school at Valverde. Now the Rio Grande has been channeled so that the town no longer is along its main course. The river crossing that created the town is merely a trek across a sandy bed.

(*Note:* If you want to try to visit this site, you will need permission from the owner, specific directions given by the owner, and the 1948 Valverde 15′ topographic map. Do not attempt to see the site without all three.)

The rock ruin at San Marcial almost seems to be styled after Black Mesa in the background. View is east-northeast. Compare this view of the mesa to the one on page 88.

SAN MARCIAL

The turnoff to San Marcial is 15 miles south of San Antonio and 25 miles south of Socorro on I-25. The townsite is 3 miles east of the interstate and 3.5 miles west of Valverde.

The canals that contain the Rio Grande seem to have thoroughly tamed the great river, so it is hard to picture now the rampage it went on in 1929. But those fourteen hundred people who lived in San Marcial would remember well. Because of that devastating flood, the town today consists only of a couple of adobe ruins and a cemetery near a working ranch. The cemetery gives the only evidence of the former size of the town, since it extends quite far back up to the base of a hill.

The original San Marcial, a farming community that also traded with Fort Conrad, was on the eastern bank of the Rio Grande. That fort was moved to the western bank in 1854 and established as Fort Craig (the ruins of which are closed to the public). Twelve years later, a flood destroyed the first San Marcial, and the community was relocated on the western bank at the present site.

The Santa Fe Railroad came through in 1880, adding stability to the town. That was fortunate, since the business of supplying Fort Craig ended when the fort was abandoned in 1885. San Marcial continued to grow and prosper, featuring such varied businesses as a skating rink, a bicycle shop, and an ice house. It grew and prospered, that is, until the flood of 1929.

MAGDALENA

Magdalena is 27 miles west of Socorro on U.S. 60.

The tent town of Pueblo Springs was settled in the 1880s as an adjunct community to the boom town of Kelly, three miles away. But when the Atchison, Topeka, and Santa Fe Railroad built a spur line to the area, the town, renamed for nearby Magdalena Peak, became an important railhead for shipping cattle, sheep, and ore. Magdalena became as much a cowboys' town as Kelly was a miners' town; rivalries and occasional violence were the inevitable result.

Magdalena today is a partial ghost town, no longer living as a smaller sister to Kelly. The old railroad station is nicely maintained as the city hall and library. Several vacant brick stores line the main and side streets. The two best buildings still standing are the boarded-up and condemned Magdalena Mercantile on the highway through town and the vacant two-story Hotel Magdalena one block south.

The Magdalena Mercantile, with a condemned notice above the door

The deserted Hotel Magdalena

Church at Kelly

KELLY

In Magdalena, turn south on the road adjacent to the ranger station. Take the left fork 1.9 miles later at the smelter foundation. The church and cemetery at Kelly are 1.4 miles from that fork.

South of Magdalena and west of Kelly is Magdalena Peak, so named—according to one legend—because a group of Mexicans were about to be slaughtered by Apaches when the face of Mary Magdalene appeared on the mountain, terrifying the Apaches and saving their intended victims. Another story says that the peak was named because a face said to be Mary Magdalene's is discernible on the north end of the mountain. For whatever reason, the peak had some sort of significance to the Apaches, for as miners picked their way over the canyons, gulches, and cliffs of the Magdalena Mountains, the Apaches never once attacked those miners working the slopes near the peak.

Colonel J. S. Hutchason was the one who started the mad scramble in the Magdalenas. In 1866 he filed two claims after finding outcroppings rich in lead. He gave a third claim to Andy Kelly, a friend who worked a sawmill. Hutchason kept an eye on the claim, however, and when Kelly failed to do the proper assessment work, Hutchason jumped it. By 1870 the town came to life as miners discovered lead, zinc, silver, copper, and even some gold. The town was named Kelly, perhaps in mirth at the man who had lost his claim, perhaps because of guilt pangs. When the railroad arrived at Magdalena in 1880, operations at Kelly became more profitable since ore no longer had to be freighted by ox team to Kansas City. The railroad wanted to build a spur all the way to Kelly, but the rapid ascent made the line impractical, so the ore was hauled down to Magdalena using sixteen-mule and horse teams.

The post office came to Kelly in 1883. Eventually the town featured two hotels, two churches, two dance halls, seven saloons, and an estimated

The Kelly Mine, later the Tri-Bullion Mine

School at Riley

Residence at Abo; school in the background

population of three thousand.

Just after the turn of the century, as silver deposits began to play out and zinc and lead became the major minerals of the area, Cory T. Brown of Socorro had a greenish rock assayed that had long been discarded in the waste dumps of Kelly. It turned out to be zinc carbonate, also known as smithsonite, a substance used as pigment in paints. Kelly had new life. The Sherwin-Williams Paint Company bought the Graphic Mine from Brown and his partner, J. B. Fitch. The Tri-Bullion Company bought the Kelly Mine, and the town expanded with new wealth. But by 1931 the smithsonite had been extricated, and Kelly began to die. At this time, over thirty million dollars in mineral wealth had been taken from the Magdalena Mountains. The post office hung on until 1945.

Smelter foundations, a small white stucco Catholic church, a juniper- and piñon-filled cemetery, a few walls and foundations, and an old vault are all that remain of the town of Kelly. A bit farther up the canyon are the remains of the Tri-Bullion Mine, earlier known as the Kelly, clearly visible but behind a sign marked "No Tresping." Since I certainly did not want to tresp, I photographed from the road.

RILEY

Riley is 20.5 miles north of Magdalena. Take Forest Service Road 354, which begins near the rodeo grounds north of town. Riley is visible across the Rio Salado when you are nearing a ranch on the south side of the river. You can cross the sandy wash if you have a four-wheel drive vehicle. If not, leave your vehicle on the south bank and walk the short distance to the townsite.

Santa Rita was a Mexican-American colony of homesteaded farms settled around 1880 along the banks of the Rio Salado. By the time the post office was granted in 1890, the name had been changed to Riley for the owner of a local sheep ranch. Deposits of coal and manganese were found nearby, and at one time there were four working mines. The population in 1897 was estimated at 150. The mines eventually closed, but the most serious blow to the town was a drop in the water table that made irrigation difficult and farming unprofitable. The post office closed in 1931—and Riley was dead.

Dead, that is, except for once a year. On May 22, a priest celebrates Mass for the feast of Santa Rita at the local church, which is still carefully

Abandoned house and Ford in Abo

maintained. A cemetery at the church, five roofless adobe buildings, and a deserted stone schoolhouse comprise the rest of the site.

The road to Riley is quite good except for occasional bumpy crossings of washes. I recommend a truck. Actually, the road itself offers a pleasant variety: because of the varying terrain, the road's color changes from brown to red to gray-blue to chalky pink and even to a hint of mustard.

ABO

Abo is 7 miles west of Mountainair on U.S. 60.

Split in half by U.S. 60 and the Santa Fe Railroad, Abo is a small farming and ranch town with about a dozen deserted buildings and a few inhabited ones. On the highway side of town but off on a dirt road is the school, which closed in the 1950s. The San Lorenzo Church and cemetery is on the railroad side of town. It is reached by taking a road that forks to the left near the school and goes under the highway and railroad. West of town, on the south side of the highway and across the tracks, are a few deserted buildings, one of which is constructed of the mortarless stone reminiscent of the ruins at Trementina.

Abo is named for one of the sites of nearby Salinas National Monument, where early Indian ruins and a seventeenth-century church and monastery are located.

CAPSULE SUMMARY

MAJOR SITES

none

SECONDARY SITES

Valverde—historic and remote, but private

Kelly—mine and mill ruins, church and cemetery

San Antonio—modest remains of buildings and foundations south of the highway

Magdalena—empty buildings in a semi-ghost

MINOR SITES

San Pedro—school, church, and cemetery

Abo—many deserted buildings strung out along the highway and railroad

Riley—school, church, and cemetery

San Acacia—school, church, and cemetery

San Marcial—good cemetery, sparse ruins

ROAD CONDITIONS

Valverde—occasionally rough dirt roads on private property

Riley—truck road because of washes

All others—paved and/or dirt roads suitable for passenger cars

TRIP SUGGESTIONS

TRIP 1: San Acacia, San Antonio, San Pedro, and San Marcial

This is a good "passing through" itinerary since it leaves I-25 for only short distances. It would be a good choice on a trip from Albuquerque to Truth or Consequences and would add only 13 miles (and about 2 hours) to the usual distance of 145 miles.

TRIP 1A: Add Abo to Trip 1

Going to Abo adds 52 additional miles. See also Trip 2, p. 67 in Chapter Five.

TRIP 1B: Add Magdalena, Kelly, and Riley to Trip 1

I'd recommend staying overnight in Socorro to include these sites since they will take about a half day to see. Add 102 miles.

TRIP 3: Combine any of these Chapter Seven trips with trips of Chapter Six (see p. 80)

TOPOGRAPHIC MAP INFORMATION FOR CHAPTER SEVEN

GHOSTS OF THE RIO GRANDE

(For map reading assistance, consult Appendix A, page 169)

Town	Topo Map Name	Size	Year	Importance*
San Acacia	San Acacia	7½′	1952 (pr[a]1971)	2
San Antonio	San Antonio	7½′	1981	3
San Pedro	San Antonio	7½′	1981	3
Valverde	San Marcial	7½′	1982	1
San Marcial	San Marcial	7½′	1982	3
Magdalena	Magdalena	7½′	1985	3
Kelly	Magdalena	7½′	1985	2
Riley	Riley	7½′	1985	2
Abo	Abo	7½′	1972	3

[a]photo revised (see p. 172)

*1—essential to find and/or enjoy site to the fullest
2—helpful but not essential
3—unnecessary for finding and enjoying site

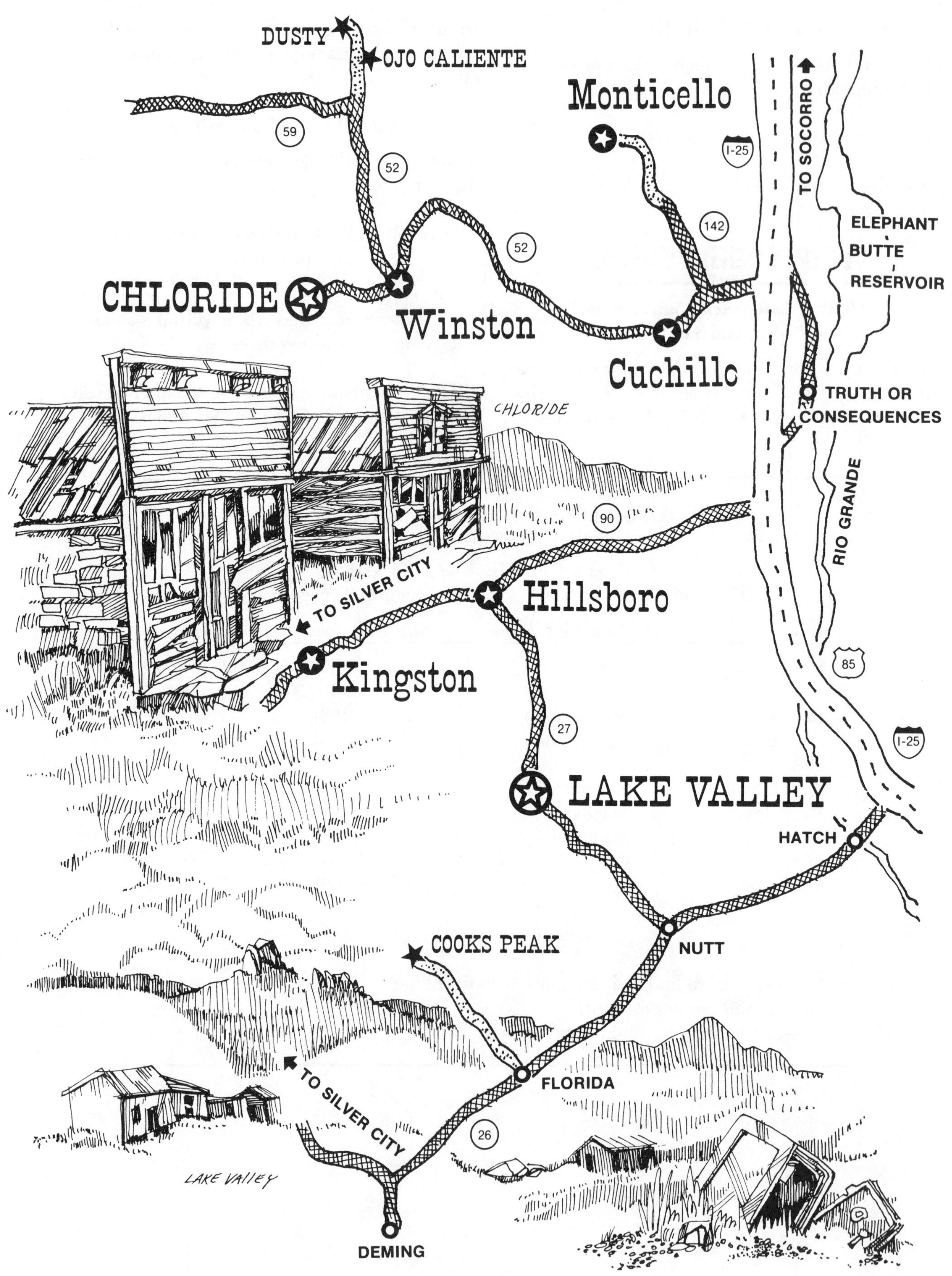
DUSTY
OJO CALIENTE
Monticello
59
52
I-25
TO SOCORRO
142
52
ELEPHANT
BUTTE
RESERVOIR
CHLORIDE
Winston
Cuchillo
TRUTH OR
CONSEQUENCES
CHLORIDE
RIO GRANDE
90
TO SILVER CITY
Hillsboro
Kingston
85
27
I-25
LAKE VALLEY
HATCH
NUTT
COOKS PEAK
FLORIDA
TO SILVER CITY
26
LAKE VALLEY
DEMING

CHAPTER EIGHT

THE BLACK RANGE AND THE VALLEY OF SILVER

As the map to this chapter shows, the sites near Truth or Consequences are in two separate clusters, and you must do a certain amount of backtracking to see them all. Several of the sites—Chloride, Winston, Kingston, and Hillsboro—stand in mountain foothills and look quite different from the desert ghosts of Lake Valley, Cuchillo, and Monticello.

These ghost towns near Truth or Consequences lack the spectacle of places like Madrid, Cabezon, or Mogollon, but they do have a quiet, delicate charm. Moreover, they contain some rather photogenic buildings, such as the falsefronts at Chloride, the school at Winston, and the service station at Lake Valley.

CUCHILLO

Cuchillo is 9 miles west of I-25 on New Mexico 52.

Cuchillo is only a semi-ghost, a farming-ranching center now in a state of decline. It is, however, much more than just a spot on the drive to Winston and Chloride, since the town has several buildings that ghost town fanciers will enjoy.

Cuchillo was settled along and named for Cuchillo Negro (Black Knife) Creek, which supplied water for the more than one hundred small farms that surrounded Cuchillo in its most prosperous days, the 1880s to the 1920s. The creek, named for the Apache chief who roamed the Black Range area, not only provided water to the benefit of the farmers but was also the source of many disastrous floods that wiped out sections of the town and twice destroyed the St. Joseph's church. Even the third church, built in 1907 and standing today, has been flooded several times.

In addition to farming, Cuchillo prospered because it was about midway between the mines at Winston and Chloride and the railroad station, now torn down, at Engle. As a result, freight and passengers to the mines went through Cuchillo, and the town became a prosperous trade center and stage stop. When the mines at Winston and Chloride closed, part of Cuchillo's source of income went with them. Then, the floods of the 1920s and a post-World War I depression hit the area. The combined onslaught was too much, and the town died.

Now Cuchillo hangs on more as a meeting place than as a trading center.The driver who delivers fuel to the ranches in the area stops for refreshment after a day's work and is joined by the backhoe operator. They sit in the marvelous Cuchillo store, which dates from at least the 1850s and probably earlier. The store is filled with memorabilia hanging on the walls and dangling from the ceiling. Modern merchandise seems out of place inside old curved-glass display cases. Behind the store is a two-story adobe barn that housed the

The Cuchillo Store is a wonderful amalgam of yesterday.

horses and mules that hauled the freight from Engle to Winston and Chloride. Several adobe residences sit along the highway, some still occupied. Next to St. Joseph's Church is an abandoned, lifeless dance hall.

WINSTON (FAIRVIEW)

Winston is 20 miles northwest of Cuchillo on New Mexico 52.

Fairview came to life in 1881 as a sister community to Chloride (see p. 99) on the strength of the silver rush to the Pye Lode. By 1883 the population was about five hundred, which seems to have been its peak. Eventually, the population stabilized around the one hundred mark. The town seemed to be fairly community-minded: it had a baseball rivalry with Chloride, horse races, and even song fests, literary readings, and amateur theatrical productions put on at Cloudman Hall (William Cloudman was the local butcher).

From nearby Grafton to Fairview came Frank H. Winston in 1882. Originally a miner, Winston expanded his interests until he owned the Fairview Cattle Company, the Frank Winston Company general merchandise, and eventually the Fairview Garage. He even served as a state legislator. Often such a dominating person in the community is arrogant, greedy, and thoroughly disliked, but not Frank Winston. He saw the

St. Joseph's Church at Cuchillo; dance hall next door

town through its worst times, even giving considerable credit at his store with no real expectation of repayment. He was admired and loved, and a year after Winston died in 1929, the townspeople named the community for the man who had carried it.

Frank Winston's house still stands today on the western back street. When constructed, the house featured the area's only bay window. Three doors north is the former residence of mining engineer Tom Scales. Historic photographs of each house appearing in Jim and Barbara Sherman's *Ghost Towns and Mining Camps of New Mexico* provide a good contrast between then and now. One street east of the houses is the former main street, including a few false-front stores and a truly unusual adobe building with a sloping tin roof and ornamental tin decorations. A local resident told me that many people believe that it was Frank Winston's carriage house. Behind it to the east is Winston's largest remnant, the deserted schoolhouse.

CHLORIDE

Chloride is 2.3 miles southwest of Winston. Head south from Winston on Forest Service Road 226.

It's what you hope for from a ghost town but so seldom find. Chloride has a genuine main street,

Deserted school at Winston

Note the curved and ornamental tin on this adobe building at Winston.

Two falsefronts in Chloride. The sign on the right building reads "Pioneer Store."

Looking northeast from the cemetery down to Chloride

Cemetery at Chloride

featuring false-front stores, stone ruins, and residences. Over two dozen buildings, most under roof and several occupied, are in varying states from restoration to total decay. Three structures in particular will capture your attention: the Wicklow house, obscured by omnipresent ailanthus trees, on the north side of the street near the east end of town; and at the west end of town, two large false-front buildings, one of wood (with faint letters "Pioneer Store") and the other wood and adobe.

In 1879 an Englishman named Harry Pye was hauling freight for the army to the post at Ojo Caliente (see p. 105) when he searched for shelter near dusk where roaming Apache parties would not spot him. In the morning he discovered silver chloride ore nearby, and later, with some friends, returned to stake claims. The town was named Chloride for the ore found there, and by 1881 the so-called "Pye Lode" had attracted hundreds of prospectors. Pye, however, did not live to see all the excitement: he was killed by Apaches only a few months after his discovery while camping south of what was to become Chloride. In a newspaper published in Georgetown (see p. 125), where Pye had lived for about three years, he was eulogized as ". . . an honest, sober, and industrious young man and a good miner and prospector. He had many friends in our camp. . . ."

The town of Chloride became the center for all silver mining in the area, although there were other smaller towns in the hills nearby. In an attempt to overcome the all-male status of the town, a free lot was offered to the first lady who moved to Chloride. A position on the town council was also offered to the father of the first child born there—"If it is known who he is." One can only hope that the lady who accepted the first offer was unaware of the second.

Between three hundred and five hundred people lived in Chloride during the peak years of the 1880s. Since no railroad came to Chloride, stages

Falsefront on the main street of Chloride

Dusty community hall and school

and freight wagons carried passengers, ore, and supplies through Cuchillo (see p. 97) to smelters at Socorro and even Denver. Later the ore was taken to the railroad at Engle for shipment to El Paso. The town survived the silver crash of 1893—but not without scars. Major producing mines like the Silver Monument had enjoyed their best years by the 1890s.

Raymond Schmidt, born in Lake Valley in 1897, came to Chloride in 1905 with his father, brother, and sister. Schmidt's father, Henry, was a brilliant German immigrant who became Chloride's surveyor, assayer, and photographer. His son Raymond, who still lives in Chloride, is the author of *New Mexico Recollections*, a delightful compilation of tales, newspaper clippings, photographs, and personal reminiscences about life in Chloride, Tyrone, and other southern New Mexico locales. By the time Mr. Schmidt moved to the town, Chloride's bonanza days were over, and he remembers it as an ordinary town filled with everyday people trying to make a living.

People are still trying to make a living in Chloride, and recent silver price hikes have attracted mining companies back into the hills west of Chloride. As a result, a few house trailers sit in formerly vacant lots while pickup trucks scurry through town and up into the hills.

Cemeteries are located on the mesas at the north and south sides of Chloride. The southern one is by far the larger, and a drive to it on a wagon road constructed in 1884 is certainly worthwhile. The grave of Frank Winston, from nearby Fairview, is found here, as are many unusual and well-preserved markers. One of the most unobtrusive stones marks a grave with two good stories behind it. In the fall of 1889 miner Oscar Pfotenhauer went hunting with his dog, Seale. They came upon a she-bear with two cubs, and when Pfotenhauer fired upon one of the cubs, the mother attacked him. He was unable to get off a shot, and he surely would have been killed or badly mauled had it not been for his dog, who repeatedly attacked the bear and distracted it enough that Pfotenhauer was able to escape. The remarkable part of the account is that when Pfotenhauer returned to the spot with two companions, the she-bear was found dead some distance away; since Pfotenhauer did not inflict the wounds, one must assume that his dog Seale did.

A year later, Oscar Pfotenhauer was attacked by a more deadly enemy. While mining with his partner, Pfotenhauer was shot in the back by

Apaches. He managed to get to their mine tunnel, and his partner went for help. When he returned, Pfotenhauer requested that he be taken out into the warm sun to die. The *Chloride Black Range* of September 19, 1890, reported the "Hellish Murder" by "the Government's devilish marauding wards," calling it a "dastardly outrage . . . done by the Red Fiends of Hell. . . ." Oscar Pfotenhauer's grave has a simple, crudely cut stone marker with his name and years of birth and death. On the back is the statement, "Killed by Indians."

OJO CALIENTE, CHERRYVILLE, AND DUSTY

Drive north from Winston for 9.3 miles. Keep going north on the dirt road when the paved one turns west. Dusty is 12.5 miles ahead. (See directions in the text to Ojo Caliente/Cherryville.)

Two sites north of Winston are worth seeing more for the pleasant drive than for the remains. Dusty is a small ranching community with a well-chosen name (at least when I was there) that features one building of interest, the school and community hall. The cemetery is south, back toward Winston. Drive 0.7 miles from the community hall until you cross a cattleguard. Take the next road to the left up to the modest cluster of graves.

Ojo Caliente was the military post on the Warm Springs Apache Indian Reservation. Between fifteen hundred and two thousand Apaches were quartered there in 1875–1876. It was at Ojo Caliente that Geronimo, under the impression that he was partaking in a friendly council, was arrested as a "renegade" in 1877. During his imprisonment he rescued a soldier's daughter who was drowning in a ditch. In 1879, Victorio and his Chiricahua Apaches were joined by some Mescaleros in an attack on Ojo Caliente, killing eight soldiers and capturing forty-six horses.

Cherryville, which had a post office from 1881 to 1886, was the civilian portion of the Ojo Caliente post. No apparent trace of the town remains, but a few adobe walls of the fort abandoned in 1882 are still visible along the south bank of Alamosa Creek. The springs that gave the military post and the reservation their names still run on the north side of the creek. The scant ruins of the fort are on private property (posted no trespassing), but you can glimpse them by taking Forest Service Road 140 on the north side of Alamosa Creek (south of Dusty). Where the forest road turns north and the private road begins, you can see the ruins, a few low adobe walls to the south-

Deserted building on the plaza at Monticello

Shell of the burned Monticello school

east on a rise beneath the hills.

MONTICELLO

Monticello is northwest of Cuchillo. Take New Mexico 142 for 13.2 miles north from the junction of New Mexico 142 and 52, a few miles northeast of Cuchillo.

Cañada Alamosa was the headquarters for the Southern Apache Agency before the post of Ojo Caliente was established in 1874. Nearly five hundred Apaches lived at Cañada Alamosa in 1870; Cochise brought his Chiricahua Apaches to the area in the winter of the following year. After the Indians were moved elsewhere, the small ranching and farming area became known as Monticello, probably named by the first postmaster, John Sullivan, a native of Monticello, New York.

Several buildings are vacant today in Monticello, so perhaps it qualifies as a ghost town. But whether it does or not, I have included it because it is a town of extraordinary charm. It is much

In the foreground, the Sierra County Courthouse ruins; in the rear, the roofless Hillsboro jail

more a Cañada Alamosa than a Monticello: the place evinces everything that makes me love rural New Mexico—the open plaza with the church (in this case, St. Ignacius); the territorial homes, whose plainness usually hides their interior beauty; and the atmosphere that makes worrying about an engine overhaul or a credit card balance seem so foolish and ephemeral.

Yet there are definite signs that the town is, alas, in the 1980s. The brand names on the store are the latest logos; a modern "for sale" sign stands in the yard of the enticing territorial; and the old carry-all delivery truck, instead of sitting neglected in an abandoned roofless shed, glistens with a restoration that is an improvement upon its original showroom state. I gazed with longing at the territorial and its "for sale" sign and with something approaching lust at the restored truck.

The road heading southwest from the square passes the burned-out shell of the Monticello School. The cemetery is farther down the same road, across Alamosa River.

Hillsboro—originally the Union Church

Cemetery at Hillsboro—the large cross has nails for the Crucifixion

HILLSBORO

Hillsboro is 17 miles west of I-25 on New Mexico 90.

About a mile east of Hillsboro, New Mexico 90 winds through soft rolling hills. A rut heading south from the highway is Ready Pay Gulch, one of the spots where in 1877 Dan Dugan and Dave Stitzel found the gold that led to the rush along Percha Creek. Four months later, a town had been established along the Percha, and in December names were put into a hat to determine what the new community should be called. "Hillsborough," later shortened to "Hillsboro," was drawn. Two years later the community had a post office, saloons, grocery stores, and a population of three hundred; four companies of soldiers also were quartered in Hillsboro to protect miners from Apache attacks.

By 1892 Hillsboro contained seven hundred people, the fine new brick Union Church (still in use), and the stylish Sierra County Courthouse, both built in that year. Six million dollars in gold and silver were eventually extricated in and around Hillsboro. Combined with the wealth of neighboring Lake Valley and Kingston, the Hillsboro area of the Black Range and Mimbres Mountains became an important mining, cattle ranching, and banking center. Stages running between the communities were held up fairly frequently, and the jail erected behind the courthouse was built large enough to contain plenty of guests. Its most famous residents were Oliver Lee, James Gilliland, and William McNue, who were accused of the murder of Judge Albert J. Fountain and his son Henry, who had disappeared in 1896 on their way to Las Cruces from Lincoln, where the judge had been investigating cattle rustling charges there that stemmed from disputes that began during the Lincoln County War (see Lincoln entry, p. 69). Blood, fingerprints, and scattered papers had been found in the White Sands area—but no corpses. The trial was moved to Hillsboro from Las Cruces because of the heated interest in the crime there. Apparently Oliver Lee was the only man actually brought to trial, and the jury returned a verdict of "not guilty" after only minutes of deliberation. There was no solid evidence that Judge Fountain and his eight-year-old son were actually dead. The case was never solved.

In the 1890s, Hillsboro began the life-death-rebirth-decline cycle that befalls virtually all mining towns. It revived briefly after the turn of the century, again after World War I, and once more in the 1930s. But each revival was short, and today Hillsboro, which lost its county seat in 1938 to Hot Springs (now Truth or Consequences), is a small, attractive community whose residents are likely to bristle at a "ghost town" appellation. The abandoned power house on the east side of town, the crumbling ruins of the courthouse and jail, and a few deserted buildings are outnumbered by well-kept homes and small businesses. Many people reside in Hillsboro simply because it is such a pleasant place to live. You will understand why they stay.

KINGSTON

Kingston is 8.5 miles west of Hillsboro on New Mexico 90. Turn right off the highway onto a dirt road next to a wooden false-front store.

The gold deposits found in Hillsboro inevitably led to miners spreading out in the surrounding hills to determine what other riches lay nearby. In 1880, significant silver deposits were discovered nine miles west of Hillsboro, and by 1881 the Black Range Mining District had been formed. A townsite was surveyed in 1882 and named Kingston for one of the early mines in the area, the Iron King. The town, which grew from a population of zero to eighteen hundred in six months, was located west of Hillsboro along Percha Creek, supposedly named because of the wild turkeys that perched in trees along the river. The location of Kingston became important to Hillsboro residents, for horsemen from the upstream Kingston more than once rode ahead of rising waters rushing through Percha Canyon to warn Hillsboro of coming floods.

It was a printing press rescued from the bed of the Rio Grande at Mesilla by a Kingston printer that turned out the handbill now regarded as obligatory in any book about New Mexico. It seems to be in them all—probably because it captures the romance of the lure of great wealth:

HO! FOR THE GOLD AND SILVER MINES OF NEW MEXICO!

Fortune hunters, capitalists, poor men

Percha State Bank, Kingston

Former assay office, Kingston

Cemetery at Kingston

Sickly folks, all whose hearts are bowed down;
And ye who would live long, be rich, healthy
And happy: Come to our sunny clime and see
For Yourselves.

Who could resist that Siren's call? By 1885, seven thousand people lived in Kingston, and the town was known as a hard-drinking place with an almost suicidal drive for a lively time: on particularly active nights, it was reported that Kingston was so congested that one-half hour of pushing, sidling, and nudging along the main street would gain a man only ninety feet of progress.

Perhaps one of the reasons for the frenzy for fun was the constant threat of Indian attack that might have made life seem a rather temporary state. On one occasion, Victorio's Apaches ringed the town, but they had picked the wrong time to do it since the miners were armed for a hunting foray. The Indians were routed. Eventually Victorio left the town alone, and a grateful populace named a new three-story hotel after him.

The Victorio stands today, over seventy years after Kingston's mines began to play out and the population fell to only 150. The old hotel, however, has been chopped like a '32 Ford hot rod and is now only one and a half stories. Farther down the street is the most photographed building in town, the Percha State Bank. Across the street is the red brick, double-roofed former assay office. Above town, just off the highway to Silver City, is the town cemetery. It is definitely worth a stop. The site is so rocky that dynamite was used to excavate graves. Kingston, once a rowdy town of thousands, is now a community mainly containing summer homes hidden among the trees. Even on an active Saturday night, you can walk ninety feet on the main street in a leisurely twenty seconds.

LAKE VALLEY

Lake Valley is 16.4 miles south of Hillsboro and 43 miles northeast of Deming on New Mexico 27.

Huddled near the western slopes of Monument

Former service station at Lake Valley

The cemetery at Lake Valley overlooks the townsite.

School at Lake Valley, Monument Peak in the background

Wooden shack, apparently a duplex, at Cooks Peak

Peak are the decaying, peaceful remnants of the town of Lake Valley. The school, used for dances years after the pupils had left, is south of the town's main buildings—including a stone service station, a church, a few residences and foundations, and a small railroad station. It is difficult to imagine that this serene spot was, according to a western surveyor who came through, ". . . the toughest town I've ever seen. I'm satisfied a man died with his boots on every night." Population estimates vary from one thousand to four thousand for a town that was born in the 1880s and died, for all practical purposes, with the silver panic of 1893, although mining continued on a limited scale into the 1940s.

Lake Valley was a place for the record books. In 1878 prospectors George Lufkin and Chris Watson found the original samples that led to the excitement seventeen miles south of the town that had recently been named Hillsboro. Eventually a syndicate headed by George Daly bought all claims in the area for a reported $225,000. In 1881, blacksmith John Leavitt leased a claim that Lufkin and Watson had begun from the Sierra Grande Mining Company. After two days and ten feet of digging, Leavitt came upon the most wonderful cavern ever discovered in the history of mining: it was a vault the size of a living room that was virtually solid silver! Miners could actually saw chunks of the precious metal into blocks. One piece was so large that it had to be broken up before it could be hauled out. A lighted candle could be held to the ceiling of the vault, which grateful miners named the Bridal Chamber, and silver would melt right off. One piece of silver valued at $7,000 (when silver sold for a mere $1.11 per ounce) was featured at the Denver Exposition of 1882. And the largest chunk ever taken from the Bridal Chamber was valued at an astonishing $80,000; that's over forty-five hundred pounds of silver at $1.11 per ounce. The Bridal Chamber was the richest concentration of silver ever found: 2.5 million ounces were removed—and removed so easily that a railroad spur was backed into the chamber and solid silver loaded directly onto ore cars. Total production of all mines in Lake Valley between 1881 and 1893 was 5.78 million ounces.

The leader of the syndicate that owned the Bridal Chamber, George Daly, never lived to see the phenomenal fortunes that were there: on the very day Leavitt broke into the fabulous Bridal Chamber, Daly was murdered by Apaches. And George Lufkin, who originally found the silver in Lake Valley, is buried in the town's cemetery in a pauper's grave.

COOKS PEAK

Take New Mexico 26 to a dot on the map called Florida, which is 15 miles northeast of Deming and 11 miles southwest of Nutt. Turn northwest on a good dirt road for 5.1 miles. There the road to the Hyatt Ranch (and the ruins of old Fort Cummings) branches to the left—but keep going straight. Beyond the turnoff 4.3 miles are some foundations. One wooden residence behind a locked gate is 0.2 miles farther.

In November of 1846, Captain Philip St. George Cooke brought the Mormon Battalion on a westward trek through southern New Mexico and scaled the 8,408-foot peak that now bears his name. The mountain later became an important landmark on the Butterfield Trail, an overland route to California. At the foot of Cooks Peak (most maps and books have dropped the "e" and do not use an apostrophe) was the relative safety of Fort Cummings, built in 1863. Nearby was the Cooks Springs Station on the Butterfield Stage Line.

Silver and lead ore, eventually totalling three million dollars, was found on the northeastern slopes of Cooks Peak beginning in the late 1870s. By then the Apache threat had subsided in the vicinity, and Fort Cummings had been abandoned. The town of Cooks Peak (or Cooke's Peak, or just plain Cooke's) was a community of several hundred located near the mines. It had a reputation as a rather violent place: one man lost his life because he informed another that lard was not a good substance to use on boots—and the boot-greaser did not take kindly to the suggestion.

Cooks Peak's prosperity lasted until the silver crash of 1893, but the town struggled on until about 1905. Sporadic mining was attempted on a small scale into the 1950s. Tailings, adobe foundations, and one wooden shack still under roof are the only evidence of the activity that took place in the shadow of Cooks Peak.

CAPSULE SUMMARY

MAJOR SITES

Chloride—one of my favorite ghost towns, with falsefronts, residences, and two cemeteries

Lake Valley—two particularly good buildings, lots of history, and a cemetery with a panoramic view

SECONDARY SITES

Hillsboro—a few ruins in an attractive small town

Kingston—three fine buildings and a cemetery

Winston—several unusual structures

Monticello—a wonderful glimpse of rural New Mexico

Cuchillo—the Cuchillo Store is worth a trip

MINOR SITES

Dusty/Ojo Caliente—one building and a cemetery, and ruins on private property

Cooks Peak—foundations and one shack

ROAD CONDITIONS

Chloride, Monticello, Dusty, and Cooks Peak—good dirt roads (Dusty road could be treacherous in flash flood season)

All other sites—paved roads

TRIP SUGGESTIONS

TRIP 1: Cuchillo, Winston, and Chloride

A half-day round trip from Truth or Consequences covers 71 miles.

TRIP 1A: Add Monticello to Trip 1

Plan for an additional hour and 27 miles to Trip 1.

TRIP 1B: Add Dusty and Ojo Caliente to Trip 1

Count on an additional 2 hours and 45 miles to Trip 1.

TRIP 2: Hillsboro, Kingston, and Lake Valley

This excursion on paved roads will take you to three of the best sites in the area, requiring 108 miles and five or six hours round trip from Truth or Consequences.

TRIP 2A: Add Cooks Peak to Trip 2

Add 62 miles and two hours to Trip 2.

TRIP 3: Combine Trips 1 and 2

Rise early and return late to Truth or Consequences. I would not try to include Dusty or Cooks Peak in this all-day trip.

TRIP 4: Combine Trip 2 to trips in Chapter Nine (see p. 126)

TOPOGRAPHIC MAP INFORMATION FOR CHAPTER EIGHT

THE BLACK RANGE AND THE VALLEY OF SILVER

(For map reading assistance, consult Appendix A, page 169)

Town	Topo Map Name	Size	Year	Importance*
Cuchillo	Cuchillo	7½′	1961	3
Winston	Winston	7½′	1965	3
Chloride	Winston	7½′	1965	2
Ojo Caliente	Montoya Butte	7½′	1964	2
Dusty	Wahoo Ranch	7½′	1965	3
Monticello	Monticello	7½′	1961	3
Hillsboro	Hillsboro	7½′	1985	3
Kingston	Kingston	7½′	1985	3
Lake Valley	Lake Valley	15′	1962	3
Cooks Peak	Lake Valley	15′	1962	2

*1—essential to find and/or enjoy site to the fullest
2—helpful but not essential
3—unnecessary for finding and enjoying site

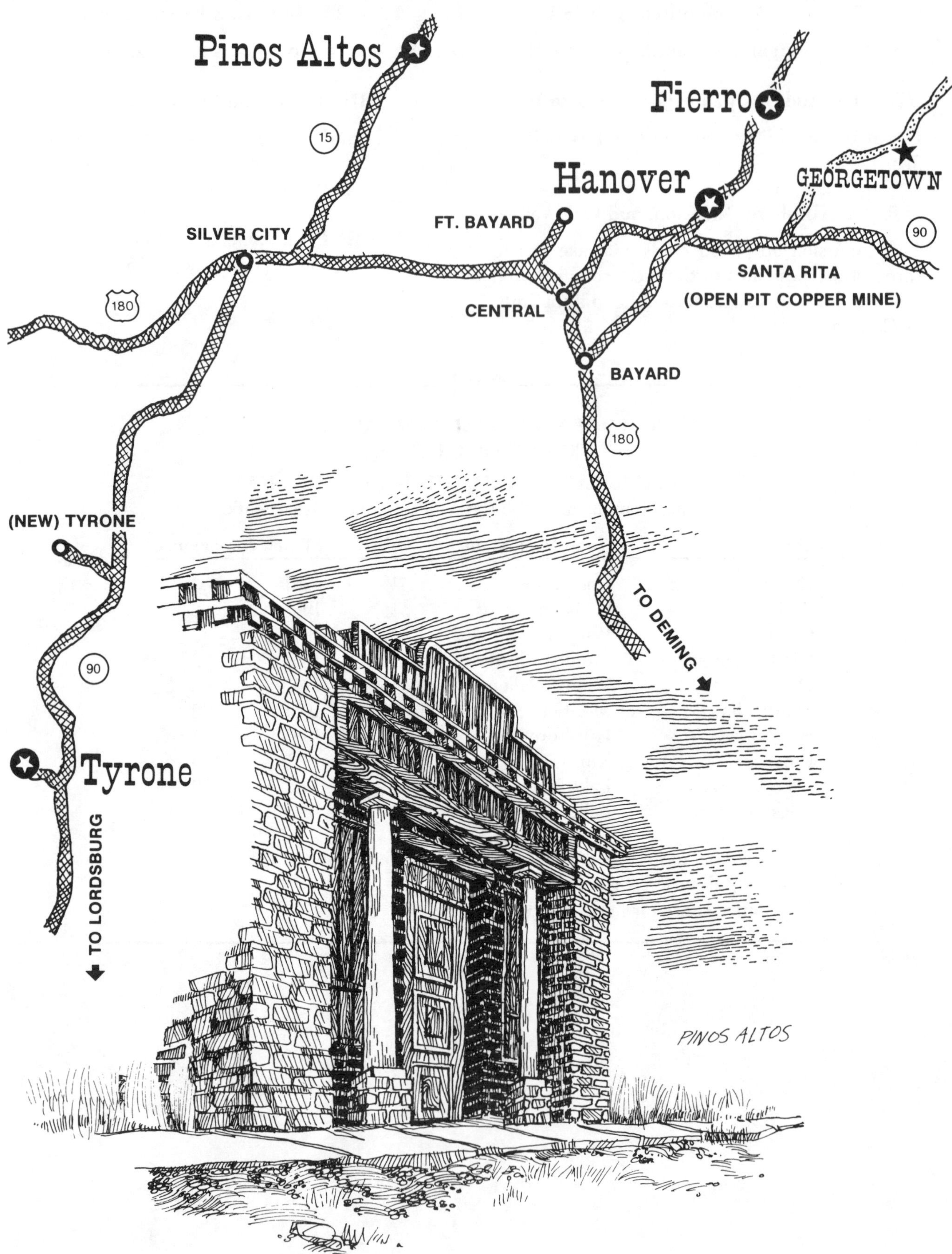
Pinos Altos
15
Fierro
Hanover
GEORGETOWN
FT. BAYARD
90
SILVER CITY
SANTA RITA
(OPEN PIT COPPER MINE)
180
CENTRAL
BAYARD
180
(NEW) TYRONE
TO DEMING
90
Tyrone
TO LORDSBURG
PINOS ALTOS

CHAPTER NINE

NEAR SILVER CITY

The mountains around Silver City contain a variety of mineral deposits; that, of course, means mining—and ghost towns. To the north is the gold of Pinos Altos; to the south is the turquoise and copper of Tyrone; to the east is copper at Santa Rita, silver at Georgetown, zinc at Hanover, and iron at Fierro; and in the immediate vicinity of Silver City is the metal that gave the town its name.

Captain John Bullard ventured to Shakespeare to view the silver deposits there in 1870. When he saw what silver-bearing ore looked like, he realized that his future was not in Shakespeare but in the hills south of Pinos Altos. In the same year he staked the Legal Tender claim—and Silver City was born.

Silver City is the natural headquarters for ghost town exploring for this chapter and even for the trips outlined in Chapters Eight, Ten, and Twelve. In "Silver," as it is often called locally, are dozens of nineteenth-century buildings worth photographing. My favorite is now called the Hester House, but originally it was the O. S. Warren home and insurance office, built in 1885 at Market and Main Streets. Main Street exists no longer, having been eroded to bedrock by floods in 1895 and 1903. It is now the Big Ditch, a 55-foot-deep chasm that divides the two older sections of Silver City.

Another point of interest is the grave of Katherine Antrim, mother of Billy the Kid. The grave is located in Memory Lane Cemetery, east of town off U.S. 180.

PINOS ALTOS

Pinos Altos is 7 miles north of Silver City on New Mexico 15.

One of New Mexico's more pleasant small towns —and one of the state's most overlooked ghost towns—Pinos Altos (Tall Pines or High Pines) sits in a hilly valley amid juniper- and piñon-covered mountains. The ponderosa pines that gave the community its name have long since gone, victims of a gold rush fever for lumber in a boom town. Principal buildings of interest include the first Grant County schoolhouse, built in 1866 and now part of a museum-store; the opera house across the street; the former post office, one block west of the schoolhouse; and the wonderful Gold Avenue Methodist Episcopal church, dedicated in May of 1898, one block northwest of the post office.

Mexicans might have mined the area around present-day Pinos Altos as early as the 1830s, but it wasn't until three disappointed forty-niners found gold in 1860 that the stampede to Bear Creek began. One of the three, Thomas Birch, was taking a drink from the stream when he saw glinting in the bed the very stuff that he had

Gold Avenue Methodist Episcopal Church in Pinos Altos

longed for in California. Seven months after that moment, fifteen hundred miners were panning the creeks near the new town of Birchville.

In December of 1860, Thomas Marston found a gold-bearing quartz lode and named it the Pacific Mine; before his discovery, gold had been extracted solely through placer mining. Marston later sold the mine to his brother Virgil. Nine months after his discovery, Thomas Marston and three other miners lay dead. They were killed during an Apache attack by over four hundred warriors led by Mangas Coloradas (Red Sleeves) and Cochise. Later, Mangas Coloradas used what could only be called psychological, or perhaps physiological, warfare: he lured miners up a hillside by placing Indian women on the crest of a hill overlooking town. Languidly they combed their long hair and performed a kind of strip tease, and many young men from the all-male camp dashed up after them. Casualties in Birchville numbered over forty.

During the Civil War, protection from Apaches was limited, and mining practically ceased near Birchville. It was in this period that Mexican miners renamed the town Pino Alto, later Pinos Altos.

After the Civil War, activity resumed near the community. In 1866 Fort Bayard was established to help control Apache attacks. The following year, the town of Pinos Altos was officially surveyed and a post office opened. Straddling the Continental Divide, the town featured saloons, a general store owned by Sam and Roy Bean (later "the law west of the Pecos" in Vinegaroon, Texas), and even an agreed-upon dueling ground. It was the county seat of Grant County for almost ten years, losing it to the present seat, Silver City, in 1871. Pinos Altos was an unusual camp, for despite the constant danger of Indian attack up into the mid-1870s, the town had a refinement to it that other towns lacked, as citizens vied with each other for the most beautiful flower gardens and orchards in town.

In 1874, Indians and Anglos reached the unusual agreement that as long as a cross stood on a

Former post office, Pinos Altos

nearby mountain, neither would harm the other. Amazingly enough, the pact actually worked, and peace finally came to Pinos Altos. The original cross, incidentally, had totally deteriorated by 1907, when a second was erected. A third and more permanent cross was placed on the hill in 1963 through the efforts of George Schafer III, whose grandfather was a Pinos Altos pioneer.

A Silver City newspapaper in 1879 described Pinos Altos as "an abandoned camp in Silver City's back yard," but new strikes in the '80s and '90s brought the population back up into the thousands. George Hearst bought the Pacific Mine, and his wife Phoebe helped with the fund raising for the Gold Avenue Methodist Episcopal Church.

Silver, copper, and lead had joined gold as minerals to sustain Pinos Altos. In 1905 came the discovery of substantial zinc deposits. That same year, a narrow gauge railroad connected the Pinos Altos mines to a smelter at Silver City. Mines prospered into the 1920s, but today there is little evidence in town of the eight million dollars in riches taken from the Pinos Altos Mountains. Only at the Catholic church, which stands on the site of the dueling grounds, can you feel the perils of the past at Pinos Altos. In the cemetery look for the graves of Effie Stanley, who survived for only nine months in 1888; of Baby Stephens, who died at three days; and of Thomas and Virgil Marston, Pinos Altos pioneers, who died seven years apart, but from the same cause—Apache attacks.

TYRONE

Drive south from Silver City on New Mexico 90 past the present community of Tyrone to the turnoff to the Tyrone mine. The mine gate is about 13 miles from Silver City.
Note: **You must make advance arrangements with the Tyrone Branch of Phelps Dodge Corporation, Tyrone, New Mexico 88065, to see the remains of old Tyrone.**

The 1951 Tyrone 7½′ topographic map gives a

Tyrone Union Church

detailed reminder of what was once the most beautiful company town ever built. The map shows the road circling an open plaza past the train depot and the department store; the company houses extend south behind the plaza, and the school, jail, and church are down a draw to the northwest. Today the Tyrone Branch of Phelps Dodge runs an enormous open-pit copper mine at the site of old Tyrone, and the magnificent town has disappeared—except for three structures: a chapel, a combination justice court and jail, and a pumphouse.

Turquoise, not copper, brought prospectors to the Burro Mountains in the 1870s, but Apaches made mining hazardous. As the Indian danger subsided, successful turquoise operations commenced, and Tiffany's in New York began featuring stones from Burro Mountain mines. Important copper deposits were subsequently discovered, and two communities evolved in the area, Leopold and Tyrone. The former was named for a major stockholder and the latter by a Mr. Honeyky of Tyrone, Ireland. The myriad small claims were eventually bought up by the Burro Mountain Copper Company, which in turn was bought out by the mammoth Phelps Dodge Corporation in 1909. Mr. Leopold is said to have lost much of his mining fortune during the legal battle to defend his son, Nathan Leopold, of the famous Leopold and Loeb thrill-slaying case.

The demand for copper soared because of World War I. Phelps Dodge decided that to accommodate the miners for as large an operation as they were planning for Tyrone, an entire new community would have to be constructed. The wife of Cleveland Dodge is credited with offering a challenge to the company: instead of the usual dreary, institutional company town, why not create a totally planned, architecturally striking utopia in the Burro Mountains? Phelps Dodge accepted the suggestion and hired Bertram G. Goodhue, designer of the 1915 Panama-California International Exposition (some buildings of which still stand in San Diego's Balboa Park). Completed in 1917 at a cost of over one million dollars, the new Tyrone was a dazzling pink-stucco, mission-tile spectacular: the El Paso and Southwestern railroad station (modeled after the Santa Fe station in San Diego) featured bubbling fountains; the T. S. Parker hospital contained the latest in

Justice Court and jail in Tyrone

medical equipment, including indirect lighting and air-conditioned x-ray laboratories; and the company department store had a long, shaded veranda with graceful arches along the front and a mission-tile bell tower on the top. The store employed fifty-five people and offered everything from clothes and furniture to an undertaker. The town plaza that fronted the department store was one-third mile long and filled with flowers, shrubs, grass, and sidewalks with shade trees. Tyrone was an orderly and clean family town with all indoor plumbing and no saloons or brothels. A former resident remembered that on paydays workers would wheel their children up to the department store in toy wagons, and vendors would sell sweet treats and tamales in the open veranda.

In 1918 Tyrone's copper mine produced seventeen million pounds of copper with a process designed to turn a healthy profit when copper was valued at fifteen cents a pound. Consider the rewards with the war-inflated price of over twenty-eight cents a pound.

By 1921, however, the price of copper had fallen, and the higher grade deposits at Tyrone were pinching out. Cleveland Dodge visited the anxious miners at Tyrone, who made an unusual offer: if Phelps Dodge would keep the mines open, the men would take a twenty-five percent pay cut. Most of the miners were Mexican nationals who had never lived in a place as grand as Tyrone. But even their self-sacrificing gesture was not enough to make the mines pay, so Tyrone was closed. The El Paso and Southwestern Railroad (a Phelps Dodge subsidiary) brought special trains to Tyrone to transport the men back to Mexico. Tyrone was a magnificent but empty town only four years after its completion.

Tyrone remained nearly abandoned until 1966, when Phelps Dodge announced that an open-pit operation would be developed adjacent to Tyrone. The town would be destroyed and replaced by mine buildings and a new Tyrone built a few miles north of the old townsite.

Joseph Kolessar, a Phelps Dodge geologist, came to Tyrone from Phelps Dodge's Bisbee, Arizona, operation when planning for the open pit at Tyrone began. I first met Mr. Kolessar when I took my University of Arizona ghost town class to New Mexico to see Mogollon, Pinos Altos,

Headframe, mill, and conveyor of Empire Zinc Mine

Tyrone, and Shakespeare. He charmed my class with stories of Tyrone and showed us a large scrapbook containing historic photos of the old town. As we stood in front of the Tyrone Union Chapel, he told us the story of the missing bell in its small tower. When Phelps Dodge reopened operations, it needed a railroad right-of-way through the McCauley Ranch. Mr. and Mrs. Jim McCauley didn't want money from Phelps Dodge: when it came time to sign the papers granting the right-of-way, Mrs. McCauley said she would sign in exchange for the chapel bell. Company officials were pleased at the generous offer, but when they went to retrieve the bell, they found it had already been removed. A rapid investigation revealed that it had been taken by a worker for a construction company hired by Phelps Dodge. As Joe Kolessar tells the story with a bright grin, "The worker returned the bell. He got to keep his job, Phelps Dodge got the right-of-way, and Mrs. McCauley got her bell. And everyone lived happily ever after."

HANOVER AND FIERRO

Drive east from Silver City on New Mexico 90 for about 14 miles to the intersection that indicates Hanover and Fierro to the north.

Hanover was a zinc town. The post office, which opened in 1892, has moved at least three times in town and now resides in a one-time supermarket. The largest structure, the Empire Zinc conveyor and mill, was built during World War I. The old Hanover school was replaced by a more modern one, now a community center, south of New Mexico 90.

Fierro means iron, and that's what interested Colorado Fuel and Iron of Pueblo, Colorado, about the hills north of Santa Rita. The Fierro post office opened in 1899; the town's peak population was likely never over one thousand even

Grocery store in Hanover

Along the branch line at Fierro

This commercial building in Hanover once housed the post office.

during the most prosperous times, from World War I to the beginning of the Depression. The mines closed in the 1930s, and Fierro has been struggling ever since.

Fierro once featured the Gilchrist and Dawson Store, Filiberto's Variety Store, a silent-movie house owned by Mr. John Oglesby and his son Walter from nearby Pinos Altos, and even a horse-drawn hearse for rent. A pool room was owned by Sheriff Mack Minton, who "knew Billy the Kid personally" and resented the Kid's being considered a hero. A fire in 1922 or 1923 destroyed most of the commercial buildings, and Fierro never really was a town again.

Mrs. Vangie Wellborn grew up in Fierro and lived there for twenty-four years, going from pupil to school teacher. She remembers singing the New Mexico state song and always believing it was "Oh, Fierro, New Mexico." She says that when she learned, at about the age of ten, that

McCoy's store and post office, Fierro

the title was actually "Oh, Fair New Mexico," it was "like finding out there was no Santa Claus."

The boundary between Hanover and Fierro seems a little hazy, especially since a community known as Union Hill shows on the topographic map but was never mentioned in conversations I had with residents of the two towns along Hanover Creek. The road through Hanover goes under the conveyor of the Empire Zinc mill, passes the white Hanover post office, and climbs a small rise. There one sees a particularly good wooden false-front commercial building, the Villas Dry Goods Store No. 2, "Shoes Ready to Wear." Store No. 1, incidentally, was in El Paso. Perhaps Villas's store is on the hill of Union Hill.

Fierro features several good buildings, including the combination McCoy's Store and post office on the west side of the road and, across the tracks to the east, a wooden false-front building and some boarded-up residences. The two, or perhaps three, communities extend for a distance of about three miles along Hanover Creek.

GEORGETOWN

Drive east from Silver City (and east from the turnoff to Hanover and Fierro) past the open-pit mine at Santa Rita. The turnoff to Georgetown is 0.5 miles east of Sully School (the V-shaped yellow brick building overlooking the pit) on New Mexico 90. Turn north and drive for 1.1 miles and take the right fork. (Note the Santa Rita cemetery number 4 on the way.) The Georgetown cemetery is on the left 2.9 miles from the fork. Extensive waste dumps from Georgetown mines are 0.5 miles beyond the cemetery.

Perhaps the ultimate ghost town leaves nothing behind except its cemetery. This is Georgetown,

Cemetery at Georgetown

a community of twelve hundred that has all but vanished. But the number of graves attest to the size of the town, and the variety and the quality of the markers and fences make the Georgetown cemetery a definite attraction for ghost town seekers.

Silver deposits were discovered in the hills just west of the Mimbres River as early as 1866, but it was not until six years later that mining began in earnest. The community that claimed a mere fifty-four people in 1880 was named Georgetown for George Magruder, who was vice-president of the Mimbres Mining and Reduction Company. Ironically, he originally came from the Georgetown section of Washington, D.C.

By 1888, Georgetown had exploded to a population of twelve hundred, and residents could boast of such refinements as a theater, a Chinese restaurant, a brewery, a billiard parlor, and even a skating rink. One tale claims that William Antrim, stepfather of William Bonney, owned a restaurant in Georgetown and that the Kid himself murdered a man in town.

The silver was relatively easy to mine: the deepest shaft was only six hundred feet, although some fifteen miles of tunnels crisscrossed the workings. A mill was set up in Georgetown, but the smelter was on the Mimbres some miles away.

A branch line of the Arizona-New Mexico Railroad was extended to Georgetown in 1891. This train service was being offered to a moribund community, although no one knew it at the time. A disastrous fire, a smallpox epidemic in 1892, and falling silver prices in 1893 devastated Georgetown. By 1903 the town that produced $3.5 million in silver was absolutely deserted. Many buildings stood until the advent of World War II, when the scarcity of new materials necessitated the use of the old. One structure, the camp hospital, was moved from the site and converted into a ranch house.

Today a small mine operates at the site, but there is nothing to indicate the former existence of a community of twelve hundred—nothing, that is, except for waste dumps left from the silver mines. In a way, I suppose, waste dumps are the cemeteries of mineral wealth, like the corpse left to remind us of something long departed. It is at the human cemetery that we can learn something of life at Georgetown: the children's graves, many victims of the smallpox epidemic; the grave of Emma Cameron, who in 1887 died "the beloved wife" of A. S. Cameron. She never saw her sixteenth birthday.

CAPSULE SUMMARY

MAJOR SITES

none

SECONDARY SITES

Pinos Altos—commercial buildings, churches, schoolhouse, cemetery

Tyrone—jail and church (advance arrangements required)

Fierro—several good structures

Hanover—zinc mill, commercial buildings

MINOR SITE

Georgetown—quiet cemetery in a beautiful spot

ROAD CONDITIONS

Georgetown—a good dirt road for passenger cars

All other sites—paved roads

TRIP SUGGESTIONS

TRIP 1: Pinos Altos, Hanover, Fierro, Georgetown, and Tyrone

An all-day excursion that visits all the sites in the chapter will cover about 85 miles.

TRIP 2: Mogollon, Pinos Altos, and Shakespeare

The three best ghost towns in Chapters Nine,

Ten, and Twelve can be visited in an overnight trip out of Silver City. With Silver City used as a base, the total distance will be about 270 miles.

TRIP 3: Combine sites in Chapter Nine with sites in Chapter Eight—The Black Range and the Valley of Silver.

A scenic 50-mile drive from Silver City on New Mexico 90 takes you to Kingston, the westernmost site in Chapter Eight.

TOPOGRAPHIC MAP INFORMATION FOR CHAPTER NINE

NEAR SILVER CITY

(For map reading assistance, consult Appendix A, page 169)

Town	Topo Map Name	Size	Year	Importance*
Pinos Altos	Fort Bayard	7½′	1949	3
Tyrone	Tyrone	7½′	1951	3
Hanover	Santa Rita	7½′	1951	3
Fierro	Santa Rita	7½′	1951	3
Georgetown	Santa Rita	7½′	1951	2

*1—essential to find and/or enjoy site to the fullest
2—helpful but not essential
3—unnecessary for finding and enjoying site

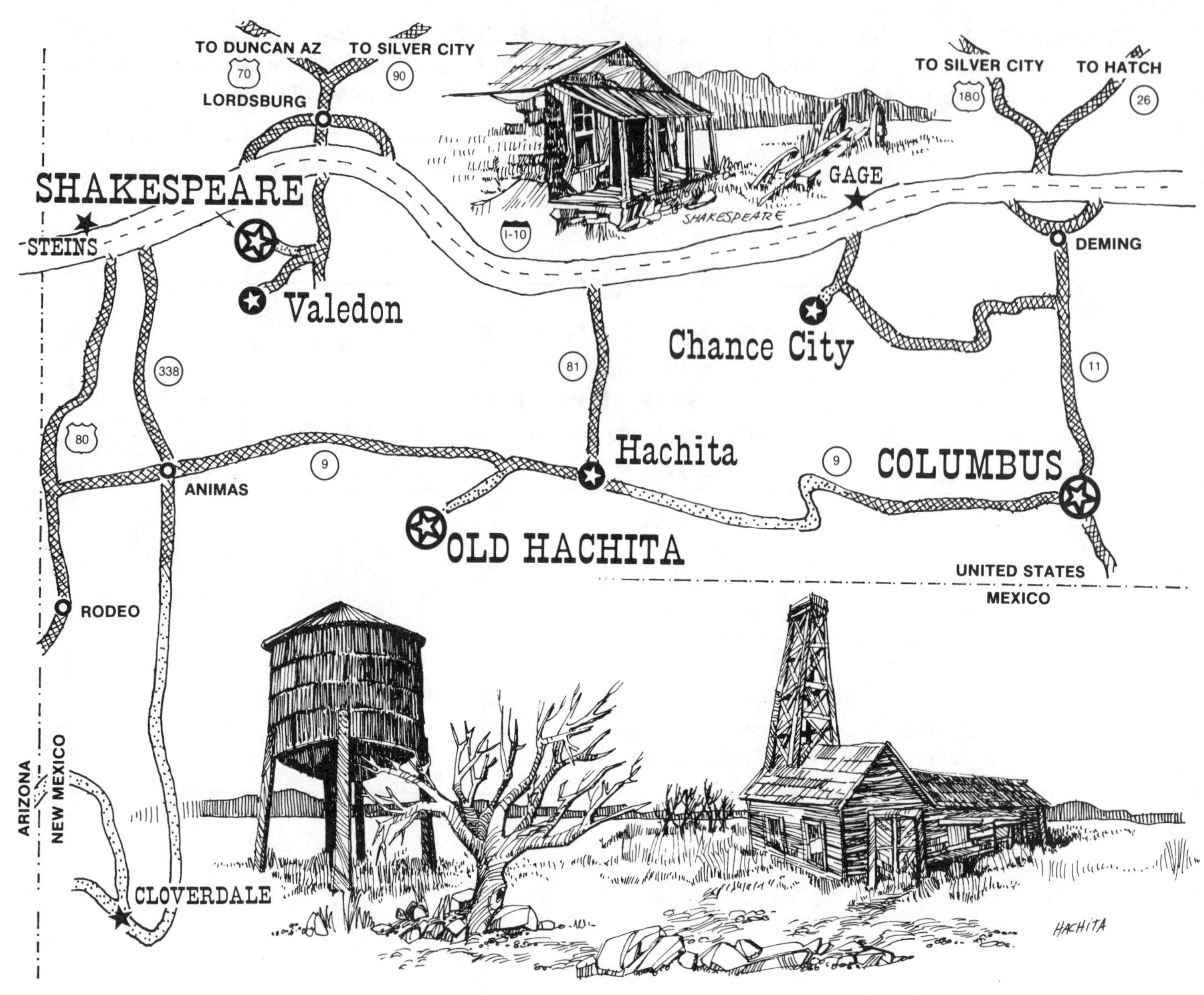
TO DUNCAN AZ
TO SILVER CITY
70
90
LORDSBURG
SHAKESPEARE
STEINS
Valedon
I-10
SHAKESPEARE
GAGE
TO SILVER CITY
TO HATCH
180
26
DEMING
Chance City
81
338
80
11
Hachita
9
9
COLUMBUS
ANIMAS
OLD HACHITA
UNITED STATES
MEXICO
RODEO
ARIZONA
NEW MEXICO
CLOVERDALE
HACHITA

CHAPTER TEN

SHAKESPEARE, PANCHO VILLA, AND THE LITTLE HATCHET

RAILROADS WERE THE LIFE AND DEATH of all the ghost towns in this chapter except one. The principal railroad towns now are also I-10 towns—Lordsburg and Deming. Lordsburg was founded in 1880 and named for a Mr. Lord, a Southern Pacific engineer in charge of a construction crew. Deming was moved to its present site in 1881 when the Southern Pacific and the Santa Fe lines met, creating the first transcontinental railway to southern California. The town was named for Ann Deming Crocker, wife of the president of the Southern Pacific. Both towns prospered and now feature the most extensive accommodations in the area.

The ghost towns did not fare as well. Columbus and Hachita's railroad tracks are gone; Gage and Steins are obsolete stops, and the trains now roar by; mining at Shakespeare, Valedon, Chance City, and Old Hachita was not sufficient to sustain life, even though tracks ran through town or nearby—allowing very cheap transporting of ore.

Cloverdale, the state's southwesternmost town, was a ranching community that apparently was blissfully unaffected by train tracks.

SHAKESPEARE

Take exit 22 off I-10 at Lordsburg and drive south 1.3 miles. Turn right on the road to the north of the cemetery. Turn right again onto a dirt road that takes you to the gate of the Shakespeare Ranch.

Water, a commodity more valuable in southern New Mexico's desert country than the precious metals in the hills, attracted travelers to the place now known as Shakespeare. A small spring of clear water sustained desert animals, then the Apache, and finally California-bound settlers. The Butterfield Overland Stage Company designated a stage stop at the water hole, then known as Mexican Springs, on its 1858 route linking St. Louis and San Francisco. The Civil War interrupted service as Confederate and then Union troops occupied an adobe fort at the springs.

Three people tie the history of this site together; the first one arrived after the Civil War. John Evensen, representing the National Mail and Transportation Company, came to Mexican Springs with co-agent Jack Frost to set up a stage stop in 1865 or 1867. Evensen, a native Norwegian who had traveled the seas of the world as a young man, was fifty-three when he arrived. He was to live at the stage stop over twenty years, the rest of his life, and it was Evensen who saw the startling changes of fortune that were to befall Mexican Springs. Evensen, no doubt aware of the Confederate occupation of the site, renamed the stage stop Grant in honor of the Union general. Subsequently, a county of the same name was formed.

Grant was to keep its name for only a few years.

Avon Avenue in Shakespeare: Saloon, Grant House, Stratford Hotel

A government surveyor named Brown showed William C. Ralston, founder of the Bank of California, some silver samples he had discovered in the Pyramid Mountains near Grant. Within a few weeks, Ralston had staked enormous mining claims, the town began filling with anxious prospectors, and the name changed to Ralston City. Within two years the population swelled to at least several hundred, with one estimate going as high as three thousand. But the silver deposits were not what they had been predicted to be. Ralston City, however, soon experienced a new frenzy. Two prospectors, Philip Arnold and John Slack, showed up in San Francisco with over $100,000 in diamonds and a tale of a huge find. Ralston, who had become a millionaire with the Nevada Comstock Lode, saw an opportunity for a new fortune. After a consulting engineer had been led, blindfolded, to the diamond site and had certified that it was a bonanza, Ralston paid Arnold and Slack a reported $600,000 for the claim rights to the property.

Word of Ralston's diamond field led to intense speculation concerning its location, and Ralston City was one popular choice. Hundreds of people poured in, anticipating being a part of the inevitable prosperity if not of the actual discovery.

Clarence King, government geologist, put an end to all the foolishness. Following sketchy information provided by the consulting engineer who had certified the diamond strike, King found the site 140 miles east of Salt Lake City (although one account puts the spot in Summit County, Colorado). There he found diamonds, all right, including one particularly remarkable specimen —a "raw" diamond with facets. King reported back to a fascinated press that the field had been salted and the find was a hoax. William Ralston suffered both financial and personal disaster. The Bank of California collapsed in 1875, and later in the same year Ralston walked into San Francisco Bay and drowned, a likely suicide.

Worth noting through this whole diamond hoax is that not one concrete connection was made to Ralston City, New Mexico. And yet the legend persists; for example, *New Mexico Place Names* reports that Arnold and Slack perpetrated their diamond swindle from Lee's Peak, near Ralston City. Just to complete the story, swindler Philip Arnold, according to one account, returned half of his $300,000 in exchange for immunity from prosecution. With the remaining money he started a bank in Elizabethtown, Kentucky, where he was shot and killed by a competitor.

Ralston City was a complete ghost town by 1875, with stage station operator John Evensen remaining as practically the sole inhabitant. Times were so bad for Evensen that he added an adobe saloon to the Grant House stage stop and dining hall to try to attract more business because daily stage routes had been cut back to twice weekly.

Colonel William Boyle and his brother, General John Boyle, came to the Pyramid Mountains in the late 1870s. They honored their native England by forming, in 1879, the Shakespeare Mining Company, filing claims for many neglected silver mines near Ralston City. They felt, correctly no doubt, that the Ralston name could bode nothing but ill for the community and so changed the name to Shakespeare. Main Street became Avon Avenue; the hotel, built using the walls of the old Confederate fort, was named the Stratford. Consider, at this point, John ("Uncle Johnny") Evensen, who in about fifteen years had lived in Mexican Springs, Grant, Ralston City, and Shakespeare—and hadn't moved once.

Emma Marble, the second crucial person in Shakespeare's history, arrived as a little girl with her family in 1882. Emma Marble Muir is the source for much of what is known about Shakespeare in the 1880s and '90s: it is her written account that tells us, for example, that "Shakespeare had no church, no club, no school, no fraternal organization. . . . (and) no bank." But the community did have about thirty houses, a hotel, a store, an express office, a telegraph office, two assay offices, three saloons, and a population of about 150. Postmaster John Evensen handled the mail duties.

The Marble family came to Shakespeare by train via the new Southern Pacific route that had been extended across the New Mexican flatlands. The rail stop was Lordsburg, then a secondary community to Shakespeare. In fact, residents of Lordsburg originally had to go to Shakespeare to pick up mail. Mr. Marble worked in the silver mines, and Mrs. Marble ran the Grant House and later the Stratford Hotel.

John Evensen died at the Stratford Hotel in 1887. In about the same year, little Janie Hughes, approximately eight years old, became desperately ill. She called out repeatedly for a china doll of Emma Marble's, a doll Janie had particularly admired. Janie received the doll and died shortly thereafter. She is buried in the Shakespeare cemetery, still clutching Emma Marble's doll.

Shakespeare itself was dying in the late 1880s, and the Silver Panic of 1893 turned the town into a ghost. Lordsburg, on the other hand, had a railroad to sustain it and could claim a thousand residents. Life returned to Shakespeare in 1914 when a spur line was sent up Avon Avenue to the mines at Valedon (see p. 134), and Shakespeare's buildings opened to entertain miners. Unfortunately, the Depression ended Shakespeare's life as a blow-off town.

Frank and Rita Hill bought Shakespeare as part of a ranch in 1935. John Evensen was the one person who saw Shakespeare through its earliest, best, and worst times; Emma Marble Muir bridged the past to the present; and it is Rita Hill who has preserved it for us. She would probably deny such an important role as being solely her own, and she would be correct, for certainly her husband Frank, who was, in Mrs. Hill's words, one of "the last of the open range cowboys," made great contributions to the restoration of Shakespeare; and her daughter Janaloo, who grew up in a ghost town with a railroad running down the main street, has done much of the labor involved in both ranching and restoring. Janaloo is also an historian and a fine writer who has published articles in many western periodicals. It is safe to say, however, that Janaloo's interest in and contribution to western history has been influenced by her mother, who became a kind of one-woman task force to recover the lost details of Shakespeare. Mrs. Hill's booklet, *Then and Now, Here and Around Shakespeare*, is an informative, action-packed, and droll account of the town's history, based upon journals, documents, photographs, and conversations with pioneers like Emma Marble Muir, who died in 1959.

Mrs. Rita Hill and her daughter, Janaloo Hill, dressed for the second Sunday of the month, when Shakespeare is open to the public

General merchandise at Shakespeare, now the home of Rita and Janaloo Hill

Mrs. Hill is also a fighter. She has battled the powers in Lordsburg for years over the way the town has alternately ignored and taken over Shakespeare's cemetery, now merely an overlooked corner of the cemetery Lordsburg itself uses. Her most publicized battle was one any westerner can identify with. In 1973, three years after Frank's death, the New Mexico Highway Department condemned fifty-nine acres of the Hills' land to put I-10 through south of Lordsburg, a move that separated the Hills' cattle from their water supply. Mrs. Hill thought the least the government should do would be to dig a new well, but the government disagreed. As a consequence, Mrs. Hill and Janaloo protested at the state legislature, refused the settlement of over $30,000 for the land, and finally erected a tiny shack at the spot where the interstate was to come through. There Rita Hill lived for three months, and from there she was forcibly removed and arrested, at the age of 71, for trying to protect a ranch she had lived on for almost forty years and in whose soil her husband had been buried.

Mrs. Hill did not touch the money that was granted to her for her land for some time. She told me that eventually she had to, to save her cattle from a searing drought.

Shakespeare is the ghost town in New Mexico that gives us the best, most authentic picture of life in the frontier West in the 1880s. The buildings are weather-worn, not touristy. The main street has cattle and horses roaming, not Winnebagos. Five buildings remain in excellent condition, thanks to the Hills: the general merchandise (in which Rita and Janaloo live), the Grant House dining room and saloon, the two-story Stratford Hotel, the old mail station with its ocotillo-rib ceiling, and the assay office.

The Hills open their town on the second Sunday of each month for tours at 10:00 a.m. and 2:00 p.m. Dressed in clothes of the period, they lead visitors from one building to the next, telling stories of Shakespeare in the 1880s with a dry humor that the Bard himself would appreciate: of Billy the Kid, who was "just another dumb kid" when he washed dishes at the Stratford Hotel; of George Hunt, eventually governor of Arizona, who waited tables at the Stratford and who "must have been a success in Shakespeare—he left with two burros."

Valedon School

Rita and Janaloo Hill do not mention their frustrations in trying to complete certain renovation projects or their difficulties in trying to keep a small ranch—the very foundation of the settlement of the West—solvent in the 1980s. But those problems are theirs. Your admission fee will be joined by matching funds for continuing restoration of Shakespeare.

After your visit, be certain to see the Shakespeare cemetery. Look for the marker of John Evensen, first citizen; of Janie Hughes, holding Emma Marble's doll; of Russian Bill and Sandy King, hanged in the Grant House, the former for being a horse thief, the latter, "a damned nuisance"; and the earliest stone marker, erected in 1882 over the grave of Ross Woods, killed in 1879 by Bean Belly Smith at the Stratford Hotel in a dispute over an egg. You can take sides with Mrs. Hill by entering the cemetery at the neglected old north gate, for that is the "Old Timers' Gate," the Shakespeare Gate. The big entrance is for upstart Lordsburg.

VALEDON

Valedon is west on the paved road from which you turned off to reach Shakespeare. At the top of the hill is the overlook west to Valedon.

When you arrive at the end of the road along the northern slope of Atwood Hill and look across the saucer that is the valley of Valedon, you may have difficulty seeing just how much is there. Even your binoculars and telephoto lens will deceive you, for the colorless, roofless buildings of Valedon blend in with the hillside so effectively that they all but disappear, seemingly without throwing so much as a shadow. The headframe of the Henry Clay Mine, still appearing ready for action, is the most obvious feature of the town. The largest building, in the middle of all the others, was the company mercantile store. Other roofless structures include the school, the mine superintendent's house, stores, and miscellaneous mine company buildings. This is all private property, and if you do not have permission to enter, you should go no farther. I was granted access to the site and can report that the buildings do not hide any fascinating memorabilia or deep mysteries, so you are not missing a whole lot by examining them from a distance.

Investigations in the hills southwest of Shakespeare began in 1885 when three miners filed claims and named them, for the year of their discovery, the Eighty-Five. But it was not until almost thirty years later that the gold, silver, and copper ores were removed from the Eighty-Five, followed by the Henry Clay and the Atwood. A

Adobe ruins of the main street at Steins. Power poles in the right background parallel I-10.

Southern Pacific branch line from Lordsburg came up Avon Avenue through Shakespeare to the Valedon mines in 1914. The post office opened in 1917, and by 1926 the population was estimated at two thousand. Lordsburg's children were bused to the pride of Valedon, its two-room school.

Because Valedon was a tightly run company town, nearby Shakespeare became temporarily rejuvenated as a "blow-off" town to Valedon. Miners who lived in Lordsburg would walk the railroad right-of-way through Shakespeare to and from work, so saloons and gaming houses came back to life in Shakespeare with the enterprise of businessmen who knew how to cater to a thirsty walk-through clientele.

Valedon's boom had peaked in 1921. Phelps Dodge bought the property in 1931 and closed the mines in 1932 as the Great Depression suffocated private enterprise. The buildings comprising Valedon are roofless today—not because of natural decay but because roofless, uninhabitable structures are taxed at a lower rate than habitable ones. Perhaps the taxman is shortchanged by such a move—but not nearly so much as the historian or the ghost town enthusiast.

STEINS

Steins is 20 miles west of Lordsburg on I-10.

Steins might be the most accessible ghost town in New Mexico, since it is only yards off of its own interstate exit.

It was settled in the early 1900s as a Southern Pacific Railroad town. The name of Steins was taken from a former settlement known as Steins Pass. A gap in the Peloncillo Mountains, north of the present townsite, was named Doubtful Canyon by wary pioneers who were accustomed to Apache attacks there. In 1873, in a skirmish between Indians and cavalry, a Captain Steins was killed, and the gap where the battle took place in Doubtful Canyon became known as Steins Pass. A small mining community called Doubtful Canyon had a post office from 1888 to 1905, at which time the office was moved to the Southern Pacific site and called Steins, where it remained until 1944.

Several adobe foundations and a few walls that were formerly a saloon, a dance hall, and a hotel stand near the railroad right-of-way today. A few

Company mercantile at Valedon

Wooden hopper and four of the seven rock buildings at Chance City face a sunset.

Water tower in Columbus just before a storm

Commercial ruin along I-10 at Gage

Remains of a Gage residence

buildings immediately to the south were originally quarters for the railroad section crew and have been used for various purposes in recent years, including a private school and a crafts shop and home. The railroad station operated until the late 1950s and now sits in Cotton City, several miles south of Steins on New Mexico 338. West of the site are the remains of a Southern Pacific quarry, and south of the interstate, through the underpass, is the desolate, neglected Steins cemetery, where the ground was so hard that graves reportedly were dynamited, not dug.

GAGE

Gage is 40 miles east of Lordsburg and 20 miles west of Deming on I-10.

Chance City is the site to see in the area, but while you are driving off the interstate, look over the buildings along the south side of the Southern Pacific railroad tracks. Gage, created by the railroad and named for a Southern Pacific construction engineer, is now principally a souvenir stop on the south side of the interstate. Some pre–I-10 buildings along the old highway are worth your inspection—adobe-stucco structures, probably a motel and a residence, which might charitably be described as neo-San Diegan in architecture.

CHANCE CITY

Leave I-10 at the Gage turnoff, about 40 miles east of Lordsburg and 20 miles west of Deming. Drive south past the Bowlin's Teepee for 2.2 miles and turn right off the pavement. Chance City is 1.5 miles down the dirt road, on the left.

Many mining towns died waiting for railroads, and several railroads altered their route to accommodate mines, but Chance City, also known as Victorio, was lucky: when ore was discovered in the Victorio Mountains in the 1880s, the brand new Southern Pacific main line was only four miles away. That was the community's principal good fortune, however, for only a modest half-million dollars in gold, silver, copper, lead, and zinc was extracted from the mines in the area including the Last Chance, which was owned by Randolph Hearst. The mining efforts there lasted until the 1930s, but the post office closed a year after it had opened in 1886.

Today not even the topographic map deigns to recognize the existence of Chance City. It shows only shafts and tunnels at the site—no buildings, ruins, or foundations. Nevertheless, all can be found at the site. Seven rock and adobe buildings, scattered debris, a hopper on the hillside, and one tin building southwest of the main townsite still stand. Numerous open shafts and tunnels dot the area, so please use extreme caution. A gentleman I spoke to at the nearby El Paso Natural Gas pumping station informed me that he was the recent replacement of a co-worker whose body had been found at the bottom of a Chance City shaft.

COLUMBUS

Columbus is 31 miles south of Deming on New Mexico 11 and 45 miles east of Hachita on New Mexico 9.

The dozing community of Columbus experienced most of the excitement of its ninety years in one violent night, the night Pancho Villa invaded United States territory in March of 1916.

Columbus was founded in 1891 by Colonel Andrew O. Bailey, who hoped that his community would be the point of entry for a planned Northern Mexican and Pacific Railroad that was to extend all the way to Salt Lake City. That railroad never went past the planning stage, but in 1902 the El Paso and Southwestern Railroad did come through Columbus, linking El Paso, Texas, and Douglas, Arizona, and erecting a fine two-story station at Columbus in the process. That seemed to ignite the town's growth, which climbed from one hundred in 1905 to seven hundred by 1915. The community had four hotels, two barbershops, a theater, an ice cream parlor, three hardware stores, and many other commercial establishments. In addition, by 1916, the town also had an immediate neighbor, Camp Furlong, with a strength of about five hundred men.

In the spring of 1916, rumors had been constant that Pancho Villa, in his revolutionary effort against the Constitutionalist Mexican government, intended to attack a town in the United States, but apparently El Paso, across from Ciudad Juarez, was thought the most likely target. Two reasons were given why Villa would want to attack the United States: one was simply for guns

Former EP & SW station, now the Columbus library

Hoover Hotel in Columbus

Cemetery at Columbus with Tres Hermanas Mountains in background

and supplies, and the other was in retaliation for what Villa considered to be United States's meddling in Mexican affairs. President Woodrow Wilson had allowed three thousand Mexican troops and artillery to be transported across U.S. territory from Texas to Arizona, and the result of that troop movement had been a thorough drubbing of the Villistas.

Columbus apparently was the chosen target because Villa believed that he had a credit of several hundred dollars with Sam Ravel, who owned a general store and the Commercial Hotel. Villa had sent a general in his army to try to buy guns from Ravel, who refused to acknowledge the credit claim and even threatened to throw the general out of the store. When Villa was told of the incident, he began to move his troops toward Columbus.

Five hundred Villistas attacked Columbus from two directions in the early morning of March 9, 1916. In the ensuing battle, eight American soldiers, nine civilians, and ninety Villistas died. The revolutionaries paid a heavy price, but the survivors did escape with about three hundred rifles and over one hundred horses and mules. But Villa and his men were pursued into Mexico, and cavalry sharpshooters killed as many as a hundred more men and recaptured much of the stolen goods and many animals. Seven of Villa's men who were captured in Columbus were hanged in Deming three months later.

General John J. (Black Jack) Pershing led a punitive force of several thousand into Mexico after Villa, leaving only six days after the attack on Columbus. The expedition had only limited success, but it did serve as a kind of tuneup for World War I because it was in this military action that motorized transport and airplanes were used for the first time by the United States Army. For a detailed and exciting account complete with historic photographs of the Columbus raid, consult Ralph Looney's *Haunted Highways*.

Small church with bell at Hachita

The El Paso and Southwestern's railroad station is now the Columbus library, the line having been abandoned in 1963. Across the street is a railroad duplex, and to the east is the two-story Hoover Hotel with twelve or thirteen guest rooms, a kitchen, and a dining room. Several homes along the back streets are vacant, but most are occupied. The Columbus cemeteries are west of town on North Boundary Road. Buried there is Mrs. Milton James, wife of the railroad pumper, who was among the dead on the morning of March 9, 1916.

The remains of Camp Furlong, whose soldiers routed Villa, have been turned into a state park with pleasant campsites, attractive botanical garden walks, and clean facilities. Is it named after General Pershing, who led the expeditionary forces, or perhaps Lieutenant John P. Lucas, who performed heroically that night? Or for Mrs. G. E. Parks, the telephone operator, who summoned help and stayed by her switchboard, her baby in her arms? It is the Pancho Villa State Park.

HACHITA

Hachita is 45 miles west of Columbus on New Mexico 9, and 47 miles southeast of Lordsburg off I-10 on New Mexico 81. (*Note:* If you wish to read the Hachita townsites' story chronologically, rather

than in the order you are likely to visit them, first read the Old Hachita entry, which follows this entry).

Present Hachita, actually New Hachita, was founded in 1902 as a railroad town when the El Paso and Southwestern headed toward Douglas, Arizona; a junction was formed at the town with a line of the Arizona and New Mexico Railroad extending north to Lordsburg.

Eventually, two hundred people lived in Hachita, but only about a quarter of that number live there now since the tracks of both lines are long gone. It is a ranching town now. The school on the south end of town is a private residence, and the few children are bused to Animas and Lordsburg. The large gymnasium adjacent to the old school is used infrequently for dances. The residential section contains a mixture of inhabited and abandoned dwellings, including a dwarfish little church complete with bell. A giant water tank along the cinder roadbed serves as a reminder of Hachita's original purpose, as do two pump houses west of the townsite that supplied the railroad's water.

Pump house along old right-of-way west of Hachita

Note the delicate wood trim on the overhang of this small adobe building at Hachita. EP & SW water tower is in the background.

Mine building at Old Hachita: double cupolas indicate blacksmith shop, machine shop, or some other heat-producing operation.

OLD HACHITA

Old Hachita is 7.3 miles west of Hachita. Drive 4.9 miles west of Hachita on the paved road and turn south on the dirt road where the main road heads northwest. Stay on the main dirt road heading southwest, ignoring any forks until you are 1.7 miles from the highway. Straight ahead 0.7 miles is the northern site, and 1 mile south is the southern site.

Stories of Indian turquoise likely brought prospectors to the Little Hatchet Mountains in the mid-1870s. They soon found not only valuable turquoise deposits but also silver, lead, copper, and even some gold. A post office opened in 1882, and by 1884 three hundred people lived among the desert hills in a loosely organized town called Hachita, "Little Hatchet." Only six years later, however, the population had fallen to a mere twenty-five. The post office hung on, probably more as a result of bureaucratic negligence than anything else, until 1898.

When the El Paso and Southwestern Railroad came nearby in 1902, the name Hachita was given to the railroad townsite, and the post office reopened there. The old site, known then as Old Hachita, shared in the prosperity the railroad brought since ore at the site was then considerably cheaper to ship. The mines reopened, and the town enjoyed a modest rebirth lasting into the 1920s.

Two distinct sites comprise Old Hachita with adobe buildings and foundations scattered between and around them. Over two dozen buildings, six under roof, can be explored at the two sites combined. Both are abandoned. Because Hachita has received little emphasis in books (most ignore it completely), I was very pleasantly surprised by how much remains. At the northern site are several residences, two headframes, a rock mine building with a tin roof and two cupolas, a water tank, and, up on a hill, a double-walled powder house. The only resident was a rather large rattlesnake. My guide around the site was young David Billet, who was having a picnic with his family and gave me a tour featuring all his favorite haunts. The southern site is the American National Mine with adobe residences, walls that were once probably barracks, and several mine buildings. A large headframe sits dramatically on the crest of a hill. Old Hachita is southern New Mexico's most overlooked ghost town and one of its best.

CLOVERDALE

Drive west from Lordsburg on I-10 and turn south on New Mexico 338. Cloverdale is 78 miles from Lordsburg.

Residence at Old Hachita (north site); note heavy-duty awnings

American National Mine at Old Hachita (south site)

Marginally restorable roadster near store at Cloverdale

Note: **Be sure to see the former Steins railroad station in Cotton City, north of Animas, and the El Paso and Southwestern railroad buildings in Animas itself.**

Cloverdale is not an important New Mexico ghost town, but the area is so scenic that you might want to take the drive, anyway. A passenger car can easily make the road from Animas. If you take the more beautiful drive across the Peloncillo Mountains from Douglas, Arizona, however, you will need a truck. Only one building, a 1918 store now used for stowing hay, stands at Cloverdale. West of the store 0.7 miles are a couple of foundations among some trees—from which two indignant hawks scolded me for intruding on their domain.

Cloverdale was founded around 1893 by ranchers Bob Anderson and John Weams and named for the clover that still blankets the meadows. The town, only five miles north of Mexico and eight miles east of Arizona, had the southwestern-most post office in New Mexico, lasting from 1913 to 1943. The peak population of Cloverdale was about two hundred.

CAPSULE SUMMARY

MAJOR SITES

Shakespeare—the most authentic nineteenth-century New Mexico ghost

Old Hachita—extensive and ignored

Columbus—many abandoned buildings in a semi-ghost

SECONDARY SITES

Valedon—a roofless town on private property

Hachita—a number of ghost town buildings in an inhabited community

Chance City—rock ruins in a desert setting

MINOR SITES

Gage—abandoned right-of-way town

Steins—deteriorating adobe walls along the railroad tracks

Cloverdale—only one building remains

ROAD CONDITIONS

Chance City, Old Hachita, Shakespeare, and Cloverdale—passenger car dirt roads

All other sites—paved roads

TRIP SUGGESTIONS

TRIP 1: Shakespeare, Valedon, Hachita, Old Hachita, and Columbus

All of the top ghost towns in this chapter are included in this excursion. Plan for all day from either Lordsburg or Deming. Distance from Lordsburg to Deming, through all the sites, is about 143 miles.

TRIP 1A: Add Chance City and Gage to Trip 1

If you are making a loop back to either Lordsburg or Deming, include Chance City and Gage. Add an extra hour and 8 miles to the Lordsburg-Deming route.

TRIP 2: Shakespeare, Pinos Altos, and Mogollon

See Trip 2, p. 126.

TRIP 3: Combine trips from Chapter Eleven with those of Chapter Ten

Las Cruces is less than 60 miles from Deming, and a visit to Dripping Springs and Organ is easy. See Trip 1, p. 155.

TRIP 4: Combine trips of Chapter Ten with those of Chapter Eight

If you find yourself in Deming overnight, you can journey to Lake Valley, Hillsboro, and other sites. See Trip 2, p. 115.

TRIP 5: Add Carlisle to any trip out of Lordsburg

Carlisle (Chapter Twelve) is closer to Lordsburg than to other New Mexico towns by car. Add 4 hours and 100 miles. See p. 157.

TRIP 6: Add Cloverdale to any trip culminating near Hachita or Shakespeare

Add 3.5 hours round trip from Lordsburg.

TRIP 6A: Combine Cloverdale with trips from Chapter Eleven—Chiricahua Ghosts, of *Arizona's Best Ghost Towns*

I often think that residents of these neighboring states must perceive that they need a passport between the two states. Residents of Tucson, for example, are perfectly willing to go up to Prescott for a weekend, but they won't go "'way over to Silver City," which is the same distance away.

TRIP 7: Add Steins to any trip ending near Lordsburg

This 40-mile round trip will take 1.5–2 hours.

TOPOGRAPHIC MAP INFORMATION FOR CHAPTER TEN

SHAKESPEARE, PANCHO VILLA, AND THE LITTLE HATCHET

(For map reading assistance, consult Appendix A, page 169)

Town	Topo Map Name	Size	Year	Importance*
Shakespeare	Lordsburg	7½′	1963	3
Valedon	Lordsburg	7½′	1963	3
Steins	Steins	7½′	1965	3
Gage	Gage	7½′	1963	3
Chance City	Gage	7½′	1963	2
Columbus	Columbus	7½′	1965	3
Hachita	Hachita	7½′	1982	3
Old Hachita	Playas Peak	7½′	1982	2
Cloverdale	Black Point	7½′	1982	2

*1—essential to find and/or enjoy site to the fullest
2—helpful but not essential
3—unnecessary for finding and enjoying site

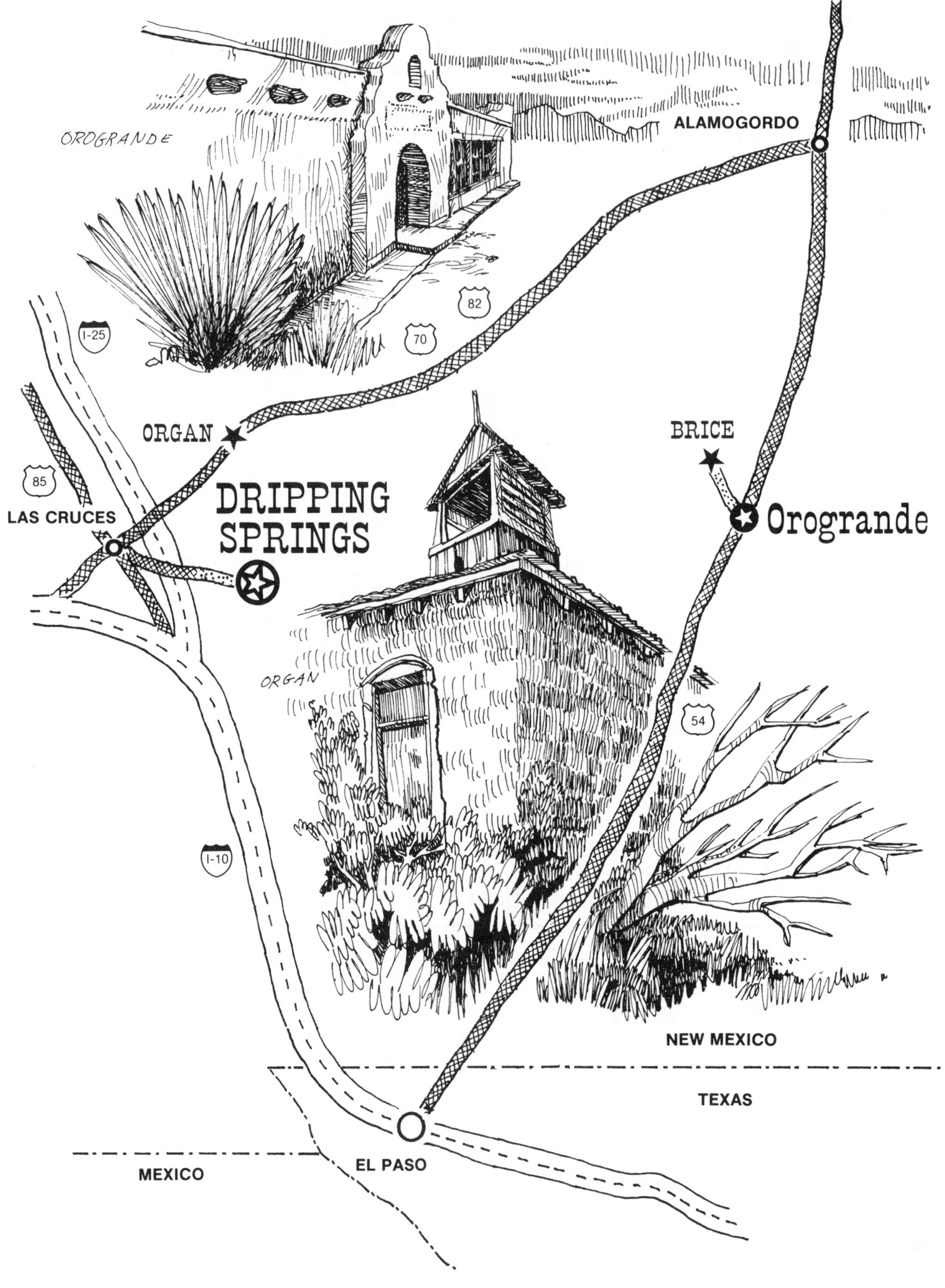
OROGRANDE
ALAMOGORDO
82
70
I-25
ORGAN
BRICE
85
LAS CRUCES
DRIPPING SPRINGS
Orogrande
ORGAN
54
I-10
NEW MEXICO
TEXAS
MEXICO
EL PASO

CHAPTER ELEVEN

GHOSTS OF THE ORGAN MOUNTAINS

LAS CRUCES, Alamogordo, and El Paso form a triangle around the four ghost town sites of the area. The Organ Mountains, so named at least three hundred years ago because the irregular peaks resemble organ pipes, are the dominant geographical feature. The mountains, combined with White Sands Missile Base, force visitors to drive many extra miles for the desert ghost towns in the vicinity.

DRIPPING SPRINGS

In Las Cruces, drive east on University Avenue, cross I-10, and stay on the main road (now Dripping Springs Road) for 10 miles, where you will come to La Cueva Park. Leave your car 1.1 miles beyond the house at La Cueva Park for a 10-minute walk to Dripping Springs.

It's easy to understand why Mr. Van Patten decided to build a resort hotel at Dripping Springs in the 1880s: the spot is one of the most beautiful in southern New Mexico. Even the drive in is dramatic, with the Organ Mountains offering one exquisite face after another as shadows and canyons alter their appearance. And the springs themselves have their own special beauty, dripping down a bluff from rock to rock into an artificial tank in Ice Canyon. Van Patten, who homesteaded the area, turned Dripping Springs into a famous resort that flourished until about 1910. Later, the buildings were apparently used as part of a tuberculosis treatment center.

Vandals have certainly left their mark on the old hotel, but it remains a wonderful place to explore. Several rooms are still under roof and walls to other rooms jut up next to the steep canyons that enclose the hotel. Near the ruins are three residences, at least one of which was occupied into the 1950s. Lush (certainly by desert standards) vegetation and narrow canyons make Dripping Springs an ideal hiking spot.

The area is now privately owned, and a modest admission is charged. The purpose of the fee is really only to discourage those mindless few who want to destroy, not enjoy, one of southern New Mexico's truly special places.

ORGAN

Organ is 15 miles northeast of Las Cruces on U.S. 70 and 82.

Organ is a small semi-ghost on either side of the highway on the road from Las Cruces to Alamogordo. The town was named for the nearby Organ Mountains, but San Augustin Peak to the east is the landmark that most dominates the town.

The lead, copper, and silver mines that brought the town to life in the 1880s are filled with water, but Organ now is the nearest community to

Canyon walls enclose the ruins of the Dripping Springs Hotel.

The Dripping Springs Hotel looked down from the foothills of the Organ Mountains to the flatlands of Las Cruces.

Old school at Organ

Bentley's Store and Assay Office at Organ

School at Orogrande

Orogrande—El Paso and Northeastern railway building

Store on the highway through Orogrande

White Sands Missile Base, the entrance to which is just on the other side of San Augustin Pass. As a result, many of the town's residents work at White Sands. Their houses are relatively recent additions; you will have to drive the back streets of town to find the few buildings of old Organ. The 1955 Organ 7½′ map is some help, showing the mines northeast of town, the location of the cemetery (just north of the old water tank), and the positions of over two dozen buildings. The two buildings of principal interest are Bentley's Store and Assay Office, now a private residence, and the Organ school, closed for over forty years, which is easily recognized because of its unusual corner-mounted bell tower.

One historical note from Chapter Six: Pat Garrett, the sheriff famous for killing Billy the Kid near Fort Sumner, was himself shot to death on the road from Organ to Las Cruces in 1908.

OROGRANDE

Orogrande is 36 miles south of Alamogordo and 49 miles northeast of El Paso, Texas, on U.S. 54.

An old stagecoach line used to run across San Augustin Pass from Las Cruces to Orogrande, a distance of under fifty miles. Ah, if only the route were that short and direct today. Because the road that approximates the stage route crosses White Sands Missile Base, travelers from Las Cruces must drive 102 miles in a long triangle up to Alamogordo and then back down or take a shorter route down to Texas and back up (see Trip Suggestions, page 155).

Jarilla Junction was a stop built in 1897 on the old El Paso and Northeastern Railroad, but when a huge gold nugget was found in about 1905 in the nearby Jarilla Mountains, the name of the town was changed to Orogrande, "big gold." The gold (and copper, silver, iron, and turquoise) deposits did not bear out promoters' claims and investors' hopes, so after a few years Orogrande slipped back into being the railroad town it was originally.

Today the Southern Pacific still goes through near Orogrande on its way from El Paso to Vaughn, but the buildings along the tracks that are shown on the 1955 Orogrande South 7½′ map have either been torn down or moved. A small cemetery on the same map is difficult to locate because it's hidden by surrounding brush. I hope it survives: the few markers and overturned fence posts are near an "authorized tank trail" sign for nearby Fort Bliss.

In Orogrande are three particularly interesting buildings: the rambling rock store, a railroad building east of the highway, and the plastered white school, now a community center, on the north end of town. Behind the school is a small residence that very likely was a teacherage.

BRICE

Driving north from Orogrande, take the

Nannie Baird Mine building with its piles of powder cans

first left turn (the Otero County landfill road). 1.8 miles later you will come to a fork in the road. The Brice cemetery is 0.4 miles to the left from that fork. The main ruins of Brice are 0.2 miles to the right. The 1955 Orogrande North 7½′ map gives a helpful overview of the site.

The Mescalero Apaches had captured the unfortunate white man in what they considered their domain. As they stripped off his clothes in preparation for his death, the Apaches noticed that the doomed miner was a hunchback, and it was their custom not to harm a deformed being. So they allowed S. M. "Ole Perk" Perkins to wander the Jarilla Mountains as he pleased. Perkins later found deposits that resulted, near the turn of the century, in a rush to the area. Perkins's own claim became known as Two Barrel Mine because he traded the rights to it for another precious desert commodity—two barrels of water. The property later became known as the Nannie Baird mine (Mannie Baird on the topographic map), the steadiest producer in the area.

The remains at Brice, virtually abandoned since 1920, are pretty sparse. The cemetery has been thoroughly pillaged. The Nannie Baird site has several foundations, many unfenced shafts *(use caution)*, and a water tank. At the bottom of a hill north of the foundations is the only standing building, a roofless concrete structure with thousands upon thousands of rusting black powder cans covering the floor and spilling out into a huge pile.

CAPSULE SUMMARY

MAJOR SITE

Dripping Springs—only one principal ruin, but an enchanting place

SECONDARY SITE

Orogrande—several buildings and an obscure cemetery

MINOR SITES

Organ—a few old buildings encased in a newer town

Brice—mine remnants, foundations, and a tiny cemetery

ROAD CONDITIONS

Dripping Springs—good dirt road (with lots of small rocks to spray your undercarriage) to La Cueva Park. You need a truck to go farther, but you can walk the 1.4 miles to the site.

Brice—good dirt road for passenger cars

Organ and Orogrande—paved highway

TRIP SUGGESTIONS

TRIP 1: Dripping Springs and Organ

To see these sites requires only 50 miles and a half day from Las Cruces.

TRIP 1A: Combine Trip 1 with trips from Chapter Ten

Columbus is only 85 miles from Las Cruces. See Trip 3, p. 146.

TRIP 2: Orogrande and Brice

This 3 to 4 hour trip covers about 80 miles from Alamogordo.

TRIP 3: Combine Trips 1 and 2

The most enjoyable route to see all the sites in this chapter is to complete the Las Cruces, Alamogordo, and El Paso triangle since you'll avoid extensive backtracking. Total distance from Las Cruces for this all-day trip is about 230 miles. You can avoid downtown El Paso, if you wish, by taking the dramatic Trans Mountain Road from U.S. 54 to I-10.

TOPOGRAPHIC MAP INFORMATION FOR CHAPTER ELEVEN

GHOSTS OF THE ORGAN MOUNTAINS

(For map reading assistance, consult Appendix A, page 169)

Town	Topo Map Name	Size	Year	Importance*
Dripping Springs	Organ Peak	7½′	1955	2
Organ	Organ	7½′	1955	2
Orogrande	Orogrande North	7½′	1955	3
	Orogrande South	7½′	1955	2
Brice	Orogrande North	7½′	1955	2

*1—essential to find and/or enjoy site to the fullest
2—helpful but not essential
3—unnecessary for finding and enjoying site

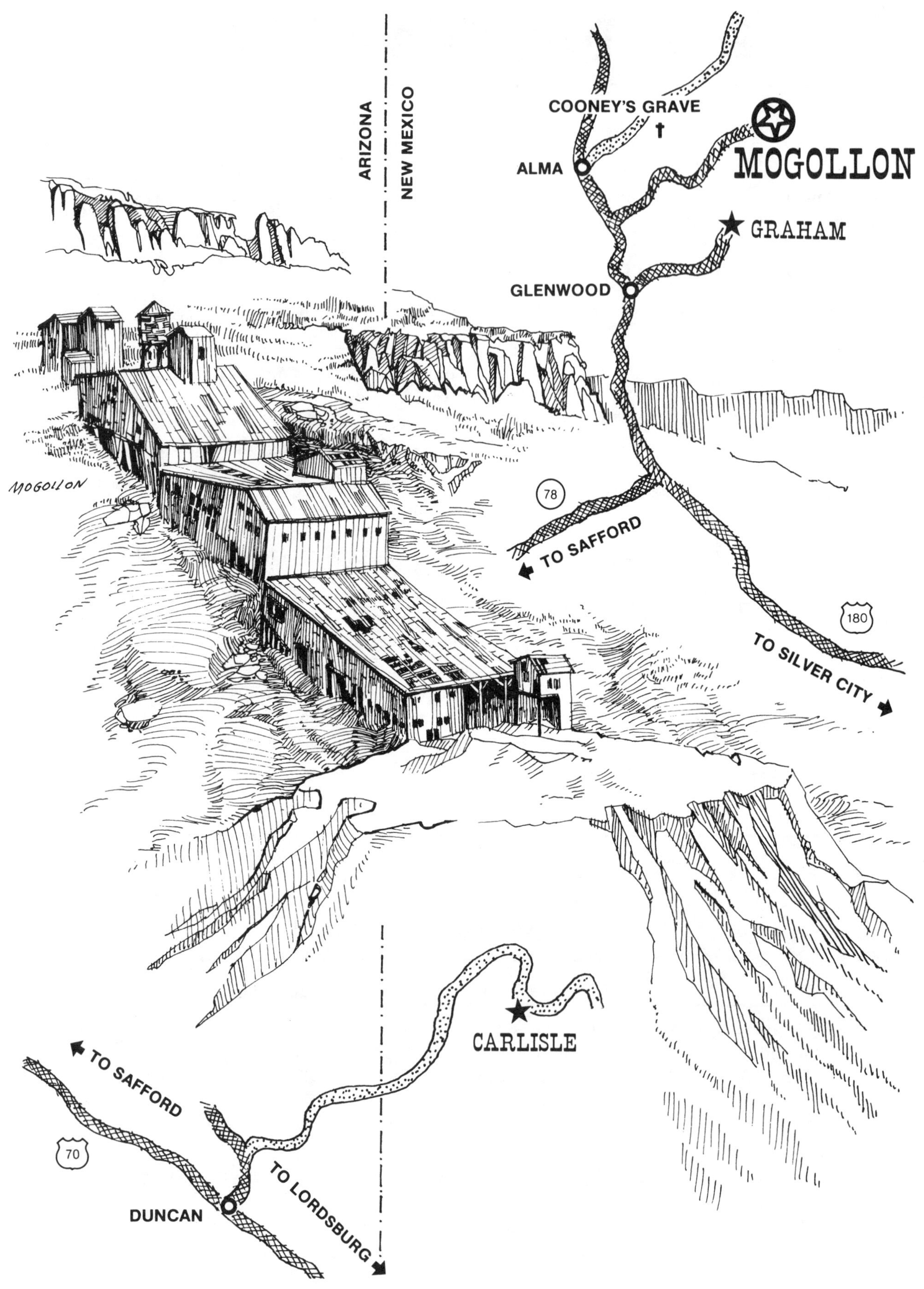
ARIZONA
NEW MEXICO
COONEY'S GRAVE
MOGOLLON
ALMA
GRAHAM
GLENWOOD
MOGOLLON
78
TO SAFFORD
180
TO SILVER CITY
CARLISLE
TO SAFFORD
70
TO LORDSBURG
DUNCAN

CHAPTER TWELVE

MOGOLLON

THE MOGOLLON MOUNTAINS and the Gila Wilderness are a parting gift from New Mexico to travelers heading west. One would almost expect such glorious mountains to be near Taos, but here they are, less than a hundred miles from the desert country of Lordsburg. And in those mountains lies Mogollon, a wonderful ghost town. Nearby are two minor sites, Graham and Cooney's Grave. Geographically, the ghost town of Carlisle is only about fifty miles from Mogollon, but getting there is a rather circuitous matter (see Trip Suggestions, p. 167).

CARLISLE

Drive north from Duncan, Arizona, and turn right at the first road beyond milepost 380. Carlisle is 13 miles up that road, on the south side of Carlisle Canyon. The site is 50 miles from Lordsburg, New Mexico.

The Gila River has not been kind to Duncan, Arizona. Three times in the last sixty years, twice in the 1970s, the Gila has flooded Duncan and the neighboring community of Franklin. As a result, several buildings near the river are now abandoned, and many others show signs of the floods' damage. In Lehman's Store, Steve Lehman shows how high the water has risen and how the merchandise has been moved up out of harm's way. A beautiful old cash register on an oak stand has weathered all three deluges. In nearby Franklin, three children died at Railroad Wash in September 1980, just a few days before I visited the area.

Carlisle, New Mexico, is only thirteen miles from Duncan, up in the craggy, semi-arid Summit Mountains; when one surveys the scattered ruins of this rocky, parched canyon, it seems impossible that there could be too much water so few miles away.

Mining in the Carlisle area began in 1881, and the Carlisle Mine itself was founded two years later. Within a few years of the post office's opening in 1884, the town's population was estimated at five thousand. It was reportedly named for Claude Carlisle Fuller, the first child born in the area. The townsite featured saloons in Whiskey Gulch (southwest of the present ruins) and the usual stores. The jail was unusual: it was an abandoned shaft, down which prisoners were winched.

An estimated four million dollars in gold went through the twenty-stamp mill during the boom that lasted from 1880 to 1905; a second attempt beginning in 1932 and continuing until after World War II brought modest results.

Three prominent Americans lived for a time at Carlisle. Marshall Field left the town to become a famous merchant in Chicago. N. K. Fairbank, one of the western leaders in the industrial movement, became president of the Chicago Board of

Carefully crafted chimney at Carlisle

Trade and made millions in soap making and lard and oil refining; and in 1898 a twenty-four-year-old Stanford graduate named Herbert Hoover was working as assistant superintendent at the Steeple Rock Mine.

The most obvious ruin at Carlisle is the rock and brick chimney on the south side of Carlisle Canyon. From its mouth extends a rock trench down the canyon to the ruins of what probably was a smelter or a mill. Walls of two rock buildings and foundations of another stand in the gulch amid the refuse and the mustard-colored tailings of a mill whose foundations are on the eastern end of the site. Roads of current mining activity crisscross the northern and eastern fringes of Carlisle.

GRAHAM

At the north end of Glenwood (60 miles northwest of Silver City) turn right at the sign to the Catwalk. The ruins of the Graham mill are 4.8 miles from that turnoff.

Gold and silver deposits were discovered in 1889 in the mountains above Whitewater Canyon. Because the canyon walls were both steep and narrow, workers could not construct a mill at the mine sites, so it was built at the mouth of the

Stone ruins at Carlisle; rock and brick chimney with trench on the hill to the left

canyon by John T. Graham in 1893. The mill town at the site was named for Graham; by 1895, it had a post office and a population of about two hundred. The town blacksmith was William Antrim, stepfather of William Bonney, the Kid.

The only problem with the mill site was that the water supply was often limited, so in the same year the mill was built, a four-inch pipe was strung through Whitewater Canyon to a more plentiful supply three miles away. An eighteen-inch pipe was added in 1897. The two pipes with their supporting beams were maintained by men who had to walk the larger pipe, a rather treacherous job. They dubbed the line "The Catwalk."

The post office shut down in 1904, followed by the mill in 1913, although some mines stayed in operation until 1942.

The Catwalk is now a favorite recreation spot with picnic tables, a stream for wading, and a path that leads to a new catwalk, a very sturdy steel and mesh platform that extends along the route of the old pipes. Water in a narrow canyon can, of course, be a danger as well as a beauty, and Whitewater Creek is no exception. Rising water has torn through the canyon so rapidly that it has stranded and even killed visitors, so today Forest Service signs point to posted safety areas on higher ground. But in times of tranquillity, Whitewater Campground, with the nearby ruins of the Graham Mill, is an enticing picnic and hiking spot.

Mill ruins at Graham

MOGOLLON

Drive 4 miles north of Glenwood on U.S. 180 to New Mexico 78. Mogollon is 9.2 miles from this junction.

The road to Mogollon, hacked out of mountainsides by convict labor in 1897, rises to Whitewater Mesa and winds up the western slopes of the Mogollon Mountains. It climbs past Windy Point, near Slaughterhouse Spring, and over Blue Bird Gulch. You round a corner, and across Silver Creek Canyon is New Mexico's most dramatic ghost town view: the remains of the Little Fannie Mine. Your telephoto lens or binoculars can pick out the giant mill, with its chalk-white tailings spreading from its base like some colossal, dried-up laundry soap overflow; the headframe, which covers a shaft sixteen hundred feet deep; the long covered conveyer, the link between headframe and mill; and the blacksmith shop, assay office, machine shop, and miners' residences that extend to the right and left of the major buildings. Yet out of your view, over a rise of Fannie Hill, is much more. You are at seven thousand feet, and so is the mine, but you will have to descend over six hundred feet into remarkable Mogollon and then drive back up to see all there is of the Little Fannie.

The Mogollon Mountains were named for Don Juan Ignacio Flores Mogollon, governor from 1712 to 1715 by appointment of the Spanish crown of an area extending from New Mexico to the Pacific Ocean. Mogollon never saw the imposing range named after him. In 1870, Sergeant James C. Cooney, on a mapping expedition from Fort Bayard, reported back with detailed information about the Mogollons, then firmly held by Apache Indians. What Cooney did not report was an outcropping of rich gold-bearing ore that he found along what became known,

Mill of the Little Fannie Mine

Mogollon's main street

Cemetery at Mogollon

Mogollon Theatre

Church in Mogollon

J. P. Holland General Store, now being renovated

appropriately, as Mineral Creek. Cooney, in fact, kept the secret until 1876, when he was mustered from the army and took some close friends to the spot of his find. They were chased out by Indians but returned to stay in 1878.

The first community was Clairmont, along Copper Creek, followed by the more successful settlement of Cooney on Mineral Creek. The first shipment of gold from the Mogollons went to Silver City in 1879. Silver City newspapers characterized the Mogollon mining camps as full of dirt-poor prospectors constantly beleaguered by Indians, a reputation that offended James Cooney. He wrote to the Grant County *Herald* in February of 1880 that he resented the disparaging remarks about his fellow miners, and as far as Indians were concerned, he snorted, "I have not seen a hostile Indian in this camp for three years." Two months later Cooney was dead, killed and scalped by Victorio's Apaches. His friends carved a hole in a boulder and sealed him in it with ore from Cooney's own mine. The crypt still stands along Mineral Creek (see Trip 1a, p. 167). Cooney's brother Michael came from New Orleans to take over his dead brother's claims and became a rich man. Wealth, however, is apparently relative, for in 1914 Michael Cooney died alone in a snowstorm trying to find a mysterious lost claim.

In 1889, John Eberle's Last Chance Mine turned into a bonanza. He built a permanent residence there, which became the first building of the new town of Mogollon. Harry Hermann moved his lumber mill from Cooney, and the boom town was under way. The first jail was merely a tree to which wrongdoers were tied, so in a moment of philanthropy, Hermann donated lumber to build a proper jail. Liquor was brought in from Silver City to celebrate its completion, and Hermann became so ebullient during the festivities that he was arrested for disturbing the peace and was the first tenant in his own jail.

A post office opened in 1890, and a school followed two years later. In 1894, however, the town was ravaged by a fire and later battered by a flood that rushed through Silver Creek, which still runs along the north side of the main street through town. Four more fires and three more

Hollywood's idea of a ghost town building

floods destroyed property and lives over the next fifty years.

When the Fannie mill was built in 1909, Mogollon contained over two thousand people and had a theater, ice house, the usual saloons and general merchandises, two churches, and two separate red light districts—the one on the eastern edge of town was Spanish, and the western one was called "Little Italy." The town became so prosperous that, to some, Silver City was merely the railhead for Mogollon's eight-team freight wagons laden with gold and silver ore. In fact, over eighteen million ounces of silver were taken from the Mogollons, one-quarter of the state's total production. Close to twenty million dollars in gold and silver were extracted, with silver accounting for about two-thirds of the total.

A declining demand for gold and silver during World War I spelled the end of Mogollon. A virtual ghost by 1926, the town had a brief revival from 1931 to 1942, when World War II closed most of the mines permanently. The Little Fannie was worked on a lease arrangement until 1950.

Mogollon is one of New Mexico's two or three premier ghost towns and certainly the best major site in a beautiful setting. The main street features the J. P. Holland General Store on the north side of the street as you enter town, with three stone originals across the street. Farther east up the street are two structures almost too photogenic to be real, and they aren't: a saloon on the south side and a general store across the street were part of a movie set. You would have been suspicious even if I hadn't told you because only in Hollywood would you ever have a combination general store and blacksmith.

At the intersection leading to Graveyard Gulch is St. Francis Catholic Church. Take the four-mile round-trip drive up the gulch (I'd recommend a truck) to visit two of Mogollon's most

The Little Fannie Mine

The wind enters any way it wants to on Fannie Hill near Mogollon.

Cooney's grave along Mineral Creek

memorable features: the Little Fannie (also Fanny and Fanney) Mine and the Mogollon cemetery. Drive north up Graveyard Gulch past a few dilapidated shacks to a "T" in the road; the cemetery is to the right, the mine to the left. The mine is on private property but is open to visitors from late spring into early fall. Shorty and Louise Lyon, who came to Mogollon in 1937, are your hosts. They oversee one of America's best ghost-town mines, with dozens of shacks and mine buildings. An entry fee is extremely reasonable, especially considering that you'll want to spend about two hours (and several rolls of film) there. Be sure to take the nature trail, actually the roadbed of a narrow gauge mine train, for a marvelous eagle's nest view of Mogollon.

You might save one building in Mogollon proper for your return through town. The Mogollon Theatre, dating from at least 1915 and possibly earlier, is my favorite structure. It and the building adjacent, once the Ione and Ruiz Saloon, are splendid monuments to ornamental tin. The theater displays the tin sheeting on the false-front exterior and on the walls and ceiling of the interior. The projection booth juts out above the boardwalk like a right-angled proboscis. The owners, Bill and Nikki English, show classic movies during the summer and also display a wide assortment of memorabilia from the area. Like the Lyons, the Englishes are genial and hospitable, genuinely glad to share memories of one of the most beautiful towns in the West.

CAPSULE SUMMARY

MAJOR SITE

Mogollon—one of the best anywhere

MINOR SITES

Carlisle—ruins, foundations, tailings

Graham—mill foundation and catwalk

ROAD CONDITIONS

Mogollon—paved road over mountainous terrain; truck road to mine and cemetery

Graham and Cooney's Grave—dirt roads for passenger cars

Carlisle—good dirt road, but truck advised

TRIP SUGGESTIONS

TRIP 1: Mogollon and Graham

This 166-mile round trip from Silver City will take most of a day. Plan for about three hours at Mogollon and an hour at Graham if you plan to walk the Catwalk.

TRIP 1A: Add Cooney's Grave to Trip 1

Drive north from the Mogollon turnoff to the small community of Alma. Turn right on Mineral Creek Road. Then take the left fork 4.5 miles from Alma. The grave is 0.3 miles beyond the fork. Add 12 miles and 30–45 minutes to Trip 1.

TRIP 2: Carlisle

Carlisle is better combined with trips in Chapter Ten since it can be most easily reached through Lordsburg. Round-trip distance from Lordsburg, 100 miles. See Trip 5, p. 147.

TRIP 3: Mogollon, Pinos Altos, and Shakespeare

See Trip 2, p. 126.

TOPOGRAPHIC MAP INFORMATION FOR CHAPTER TWELVE

MOGOLLON

(For map reading assistance, consult Appendix A, page 169)

Town	Topo Map Name	Size	Year	Importance*
Carlisle	Steeple Rock	15′	1959	2
Graham	Mogollon	7½′	1963	3
Mogollon	Mogollon	7½′	1963	2
Cooney's Grave	Mogollon	7½′	1963	3

*1—essential to find and/or enjoy site to the fullest
2—helpful but not essential
3—unnecessary for finding and enjoying site

APPENDIXES

APPENDIX A: READING TOPOGRAPHIC MAPS

A topographic map is a representation of natural and manmade features of a portion of the earth plotted to a specific scale. It shows locations and shapes of mountains, valleys, rivers, and lakes as well as principal works of man.

For the ghost town enthusiast, the topographic map (or "topo" or "quad") is a particularly valuable aid in locating towns in remote areas, determining where mines were near those towns, and noting what buildings or ruins were at the site when the map was made. Topographic maps are more valuable than highway maps because they are so much more detailed. Nevertheless, some are more essential than others—although all are useful. In many cases the maps in this book are all you will need for outings. But be certain to check the Topographic Map Information pages for the various chapters before you go.

15 Minute and 7½ Minute

The two map sizes you will encounter most frequently are 15 minute and 7½ minute maps. There are 360 degrees of latitude and longitude to the earth and 60 minutes to each degree. A 15′ map covers one-fourth of a degree of latitude or longitude; sixteen 15′ maps cover one degree of latitude and one degree of longitude. A 7½′ map, which is larger in size than a 15′ map, actually covers only one-fourth the area of a 15′ map.

As a result, the 7½′ is much more detailed and usually far more helpful to the ghost-town hunter. In a 15′ map, one inch represents about one mile; in a 7½′, one inch represents about two thousand feet. Since a 7½′ covers such a small area, you must use several to cover a part of the state filled with ghost towns if you want maps for them all. For example, I consulted fourteen for the towns in the Madrid area. But if you will consult the Topographic Map Information for Chapter One, page 13, you will discover that only one map is essential since you have this book; and only one other is recommended as helpful but not essential in enhancing your enjoyment of the site.

Generally, the 15′ maps are older. The U.S. Geological Survey has been replacing many of the 15′ maps with four 7½′ maps when new surveys are made. Nevertheless, the older maps can be quite valuable since a topographic map from 1947 will show what was there decades ago, so the real adventurer can scour the area for nearly vanished roads and decaying foundations that are not apparent to the casual visitor.

Distinguishing Characteristics

The primary feature of a topographic map that is unfamiliar to the average person is the brown contour lines that extend throughout the map. These show steepness of slope. Quite simply, where the contour lines are close together the grade is steep; where they are far apart the land

Area Covered by Maps

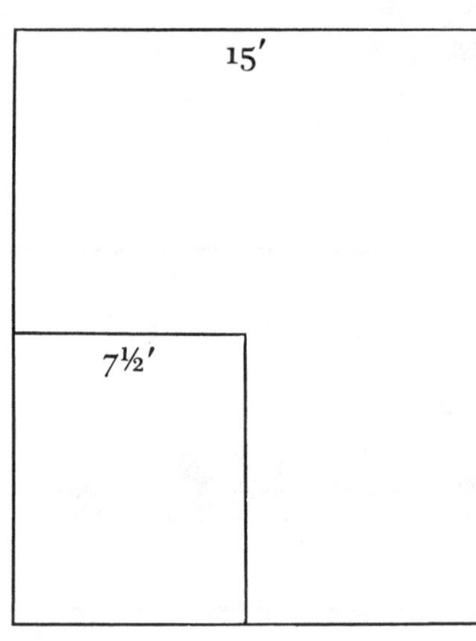

Size Comparison of Maps
(shown at 1/10 their actual size)

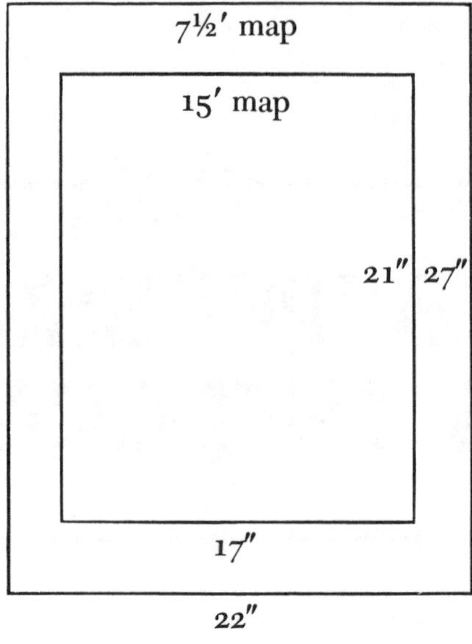

is fairly level. You may have had the experience when traveling a back road of following the gently curving line on the highway map only to discover that it is a dangerous, mountainous route. A topographic map clearly shows the terrain, so you should have a much clearer picture of the road ahead.

Another unfamiliar feature is the red lines that crisscross the map. They are particularly helpful in estimating distance since each section they mark off is one square mile. Not all areas, however, have been surveyed for square-mile sections.

The final unfamiliar feature of the topographic map is the presence of numbers like "R. 8 E." and "T. 22 S." These refer to the map's location relative to the initial point of reference of New Mexico maps, a point just northeast of the town of San Acacia, on a hill on the west bank of the Rio Grande (see San Acacia entry, page 83). At that point the New Mexico Baseline (east and west) intersects the New Mexico Principal Meridian (north and south), and all points on topographic maps of New Mexico are surveyed relative to that spot.

The notations R. 8 E. and T. 22 S. indicate a place in the eighth range east of the Meridian and the twenty-second township south of the Baseline. A township-range is an area six miles by six miles usually subdivided into thirty-six sections of one square mile each. In R. 8 E. and T. 22 S. are the ghost towns of Orogrande and Brice.

The margins of a topographic map contain useful information such as the scale, showing distances; the date the map was made; the location of the quadrangle of which this map is a part; the difference between true and magnetic north when the map was made; and very importantly, the names of the eight maps that border the map you have. The name of the map, incidentally, is chosen because of a prominent feature, either natural or manmade, on that map.

Availability

Topographic maps are available at many blueprint shops, hunters' or hikers' supply stores, and some bookstores. Instead of buying maps, however, you might consider simply examining them at a university library. The University of Arizona, for example, has a complete selection of topographic maps for all fifty states. Nearby is a photocopying machine that I used for over two hundred pages of maps of New Mexico. (U.S. Geological Survey maps are in the public domain, and photocopying is perfectly legal.) I spent two hundred nickels photocopying 126 maps instead of paying about $200 to buy them. The copies do lose something compared to the original since they are not in color, but I did not find that to be detrimental while in the field. The University

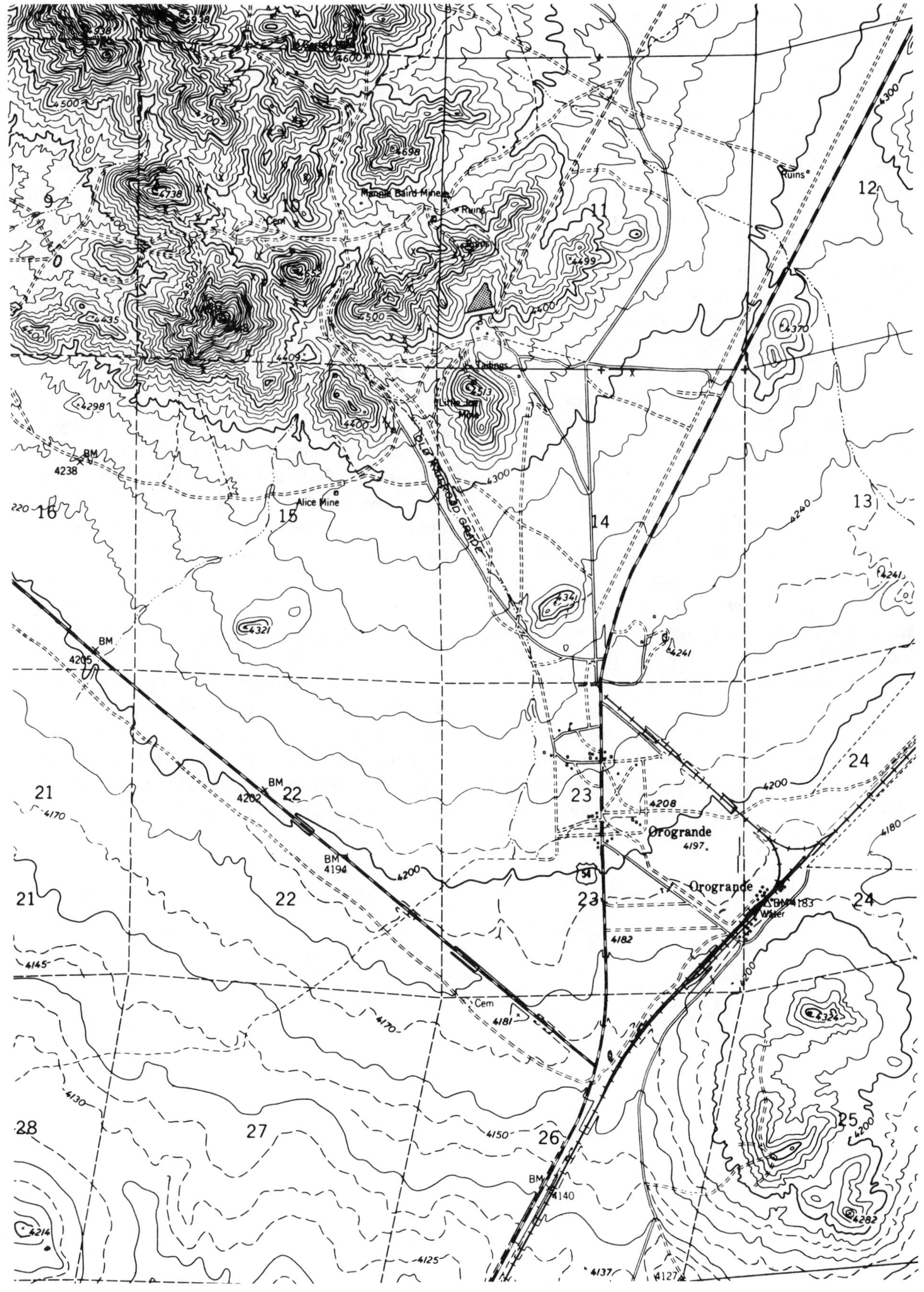

Manning Baird Mine
Ruins
Cem
Tailings
Little Lone Mtn
Alice Mine
OLD RAILROAD GRADE
Orogrande
Water
Cem

of New Mexico, incidentally, also has a complete set of topographic maps and a nearby photocopying machine.

While at the library, consult an index that shows all the topographic maps available for New Mexico and a topographic symbols sheet that details the various lines, colors, and symbols used in the maps. If you decide to buy maps, you can cut the cost by ordering from the U.S. Geological Survey rather than by buying them from a retail store. The address:

Branch of Distribution
U.S. Geological Survey
Box 25286, Federal Center
Denver, Colorado 80225

A handy brochure that I consulted for this appendix is "Topographic Maps" by Theodore D. Steger, available without charge at some U.S. Geological Survey offices.

Comparing Maps

A highway map is well suited for getting you around New Mexico on major roads, but it is not suited for ghost town hunting on the back roads since it will not include minor roads and will not indicate the terrain that the roads must traverse. Only a topographic map will provide what is often essential information.

A portion of the 1940 15′ Orogrande topographic map (see p. 170) shows an area of about 4.2 miles north to south and 3 miles east to west. The map shows the town of Orogrande, only a small dot on a highway map, with actual locations of buildings. The contour lines show the rise in altitude northwest of town out to the site of Brice, marked by the Nannie Baird Mine.

Portions of two 7½′ maps, the 1955 Orogrande North and the 1955 Orogrande South, need to be combined to show the same area (see p. 171) as the 15′ map. The map is much larger for the same area and is in considerably more detail. The tiny Orogrande and Brice cemeteries, not on the 15′ map, are visible (in sections 10 and 26). Minor roads and trails are also included, as well as the old railroad grade from Orogrande to the Brice area. Note the discrepancy: the Nannie Baird Mine is called the Nannie Beard on the 15′ and the Mannie Baird on the 7½′.

The map for Chapter Eleven of this book (see page 148) includes the same areas as these topographic maps. Coupled with the directions included in the individual entries, this map is more useful than a highway map but far less detailed than the topographic maps. For the person who wishes to see more at a site than the obvious and to explore more of the area to get a real feeling for what once was there, the topographic map is an irreplaceable aid.

NOTE: Several topographic maps mentioned at the end of chapters are labeled "photorevised." This means that a map originally drawn in one year has been updated at a later date with aerial photographs because of interstate highways, dams, or other major projects.

APPENDIX B: GLOSSARY OF FREQUENTLY USED MINING TERMS

ADIT: A horizontal or nearly horizontal entrance to a mine; a tunnel.

CHARCOAL OVEN: Structure into which wood is placed and subjected to intense heat, resulting in charcoal. Charcoal is a long-lasting, efficient wood fuel often used to power mills and smelters.

COKE OVEN: Same as above, only coal is used to produce coke. Coke then burns longer and hotter than coal and is used for power in mills and smelters.

HEADFRAME: The vertical apparatus over a mine shaft that has cables to be lowered down the shaft for the raising of ore; sometimes called a "gallows frame."

MILL: A building in which rock is crushed to extricate minerals; usually constructed on the side of a hill—hence, a "gravity-feed" mill.

PLACER: A waterborne deposit of sand or gravel containing heavier materials like gold that have been eroded from their original bedrock and concentrated as small particles that can be washed out.

SHAFT: A vertical or nearly vertical opening into the earth for mining.

SMELTER: A building or complex in which material is melted so as to separate impurities from pure metal.

STAMP MILL: A machine that pulverizes ore by means of heavy hammers or pestles, called "stamps."

TAILINGS: Waste or refuse left after milling is complete; sometimes used more generally to include waste dumps.

WASTE DUMP: Waste rock that comes out of the mine; rock that is not of sufficient value to warrant milling.

APPENDIX C: PRONUNCIATION GUIDE

Most New Mexicans and Spanish-speaking readers will find much of this appendix superfluous. Hundreds of Spanish words, naturally, appear in this book, but I have only included the pronunciation of those words (almost all of them Spanish) that are likely to be used when talking to people about the sites. It is, after all, somewhat embarrassing to speak with a resident of a town and mispronounce the name of his home. Spanish words are given in a somewhat anglicized form, the form native Anglos tend to use.

Abo—*ay*-boh
Ancho—*ahn*-choe
Animas—*an*-ih-muss
Cabezon—kah-beh-*zohn*
Carrizozo—kair-ih-*soe*-soe
Castañeda—kah-stah-*nyay*-duh
Cerrillos—sair-*ree*-ohse
Chiricahua—cheer-uh-*kah*-wah
Cimarron—see-muh-*rone* (or, more commonly anglicized to *sim*-uh-ron)
Colonias—koh-*lone*-ee-us
Coyote—ko-*yoh*-teh
Cuchillo—koo-*chee*-oh
Cuervo—*kwair*-voe
Evensen—*eh*-ven-sen
Fierro—fee-*air*-oh
Galisteo—gah-lis-*stay*-oh
Gamerco—guh-*mair*-koe
Gila—*hee*-luh
Hachita—hah-*chee*-tuh
Jarilla—hah-*ree*-uh
Jicarilla—hee-kah-*ree*-uh
Jornada del Muerto—hore-*nah*-thuh-dell-*mwair*-toh
Koehler—*kay*-ler
Kolessar—kuh-*less*-er
La Bajada—la-bah-*hah*-thah
La Cueva—lah-*kway*-vuh
La Junta—lah-*hoon*-tah
La Liendre—lah-lee-*en*-dray
Lamy—*lay*-mee
Loma Parda—*loh*-mah-*par*-dah
Madrid—*ma* ("a" as in "hat")-drid (also occasionally *mah*-drid)
Mangas Coloradas—*mang*-gus-koh-loh-*rah*-das
Mescalero—mess-kah-*lair*-oh
Mimbres—*mim*-bress
Mogollon—mug-ee-*ohn*
Ojo Caliente—*oh*-hoe-kahl-yee-*en*-tay
Orogrande—ore-oh-*grahn*-day
Ortiz—ore-*tees*
Peloncillo—pell-ohn-*see*-oh
Percha—*perch*-uh
Pinos Altos—*pee*-nohs-*awl*-tose
Placer—*plass*-er
Puerto de Luna—*pwair*-toh-day-*loon*-uh
Raton—rah-*tone* or ra-*tone*
Rayado—rye-*ay*-thoe
Reventon—*ray*-ven-tun
Rio Grande—*ree*-oh-*grahn*-day
Rio Puerco—*ree*-oh-*pwair*-koh
Rio Salado—*ree*-oh-sah-*lah*-thoe
San Acacia—sahn-ah-*kah*-see-uh
San Geronimo—sahn-her-*ahn*-uh-moh
San Marcial—sahn-mar-see-*all*
Sangre de Cristo—*sahn*-gray-day-*cree*-stoh
Socorro—suh-*kore*-oh
Steins—*steenz*
Sugarite—shug-er-*eet*
Trementina—*tray*-men-*tee*-nuh
Tuerto—*twair*-toe
Valedon—*vail*-dun or val-uh-*dohn*
Valverde—val-*vair*-day
Watrous—*watt*-russ
Yaksich—*yak*-sick
Yeso—*yay*-soh

APPENDIX D: PHOTOGRAPHING GHOST TOWNS

Consider one certainty: film is cheap compared to gasoline. Consider one probability: you may never return to a particular ghost town, and even if you do, it will not look the same the second time. For these reasons, take along a camera and plenty of film.

The Camera

Any old camera is certainly better than no camera on a ghost town outing, but the person who insists, "I can take just as good a picture with my pocket camera as I could with a fancy camera" simply isn't correct. If the pictures please him, that is all that really matters. But better cameras do take better pictures because their lenses are more precisely ground and because they are infinitely more versatile with their varying shutter speeds and apertures. With the advent of "automatic" single lens reflex cameras, the quality photograph is now virtually as easy to take as the "pocket" photograph is.

In suggesting what camera to use, professionals will likely give the nod to what are called medium- and large-format cameras. But the most popular quality camera on the market, and perhaps the most practical, is the 35mm single lens reflex (SLR) camera. Since it is popular and relatively affordable and since it is my personal choice, I will suggest equipment based on an SLR system. An SLR allows you to take excellent photographs with the initial investment as well as add lenses and other accessories when you become more sophisticated and demanding with your camera.

The Accessories

- In addition to the 50mm lens usually standard with an SLR, the most important lens for ghost-towning is a 28mm or 35mm wide angle lens. This lens is particularly valuable for showing interiors of buildings and for conveying the look of the overall site.
- A third lens that often allows the photographer the only real look at a site (e.g., if it is closed to visitors or on a distant cliff) is the telephoto, a lens of 135mm or more. You might consider a telephoto zoom lens for the same purpose. Photographs taken with a high-quality zoom are indistinguishable from other telephotos for the purposes of most photographers. Several photographs in this volume were taken with a telephoto zoom.
- A lens that I have found tremendously useful (albeit expensive) is a relatively new item in lenses, a zoom that goes from wide angle to short telephoto. Mine is a 28mm to 85mm, and it allows a remarkable range of shots without changing lenses. Purists may scoff at such a lens, but I have had beautiful results. Many of the color photographs and a few of the black and whites in this book were taken with this versatile lens.
- Use an ultraviolet (UV) haze filter or a skylight filter on any of your lenses for two reasons: they protect the lens itself from damage, and they correct for excessive bluishness in the outdoors.
- If you don't have macro capabilities on a lens, buy a close-up lens set. It's very inexpensive and allows you to photograph all sorts of details at a site such as buttons, hinges, tin, glass, and ornamental iron.
- A tripod permits low-light photography, such as in mines, interiors of buildings, and dawn and dusk photos. It also permits you to be in your own pictures if your camera has a self-timer.
- For those occasions when a tripod is too slow, too bulky, or too heavy, carry an electronic flash. I have a small pocket-sized flash on hikes, and a large thyristor-type flash stays in my case in the car.
- Speaking of cases—a camera bag or case is an

essential piece of equipment, not an accessory. You will be driving over miles of back roads, and dust is a camera's worst enemy. Most bags do an acceptable job of keeping out dust; aluminum cases, such as a Halliburton, are virtually dust-proof but are expensive. Incidentally, in addition to keeping your camera away from dust, also keep it and your spare film out of prolonged direct sunlight or heat, such as baking in the car for hour after hour. A moisture-proof pouch kept in your cooler is a wise choice for film.

Film

Slide film has advantages over print film for ghost town enthusiasts. It is cheaper per frame, and it is easier to show your pictures with a projector than to pass them around to friends. In addition, since your slide is the processed film itself, what you see is what you took; no error should be made in cropping by the photo lab, a problem that occurs often with print film. Finally, those especially good slides can be made into prints of very good quality. Print film does have the advantage that it is a better quality print than a print from a slide, and naturally, print film does not require the expense of a projector.

I prefer Ektachrome over Kodachrome because the color is more true to the actual scene; Kodachrome gives the more splendid, more dramatic results because of its emphasis on reds and browns, but I find it a bit dishonest—often the photographs are more beautiful than the scenes themselves were. My purpose, as I see it, is to record the sites as accurately as possible. If your purpose is different, choose your film accordingly. In addition, Ektachrome is available in a much wider range of film speeds. All color photographs in this book were originally Ektachrome slides.

How much film should you have with you? This varies enormously depending upon your desire to record the site. My rule of thumb is: take along twice as much film as you could possibly imagine yourself shooting. That way, when you come across something truly spectacular (and it will happen), you won't have to worry about rationing out film for the whole day.

Suggestions for Technique

- Perhaps the first rule is: know your camera and its capabilities by studying the manual and experimenting with the camera. You might also be wise to buy an inexpensive book on photography to learn about techniques like backlighting, bracketing, multiple exposure, and others.
- If your reason for taking a camera is to show others and remind yourself what the ghost town looks like, try to take some pictures that give a feeling of the totality of the site. You can do this by either taking pictures from a hill or by including in several pictures a common reference point, such as a church steeple, smelter stack, or large ruin. Then, when showing your pictures, you can help the viewer get a better image of the town by saying "just north of that smelter stack" or "to the west of that same building is this adobe ruin," and so on.
- While looking at the large—the headframes of mines, the tailings, the buildings—don't overlook the small—weathered wood, a rusted hinge—which may offer the most intriguing and personally satisfying photos. Cemeteries, for example, often contain many details worth examining.
- If you have *Ghost Towns and Mining Camps of New Mexico*, *Haunted Highways*, or other texts that include historical photographs, it's interesting to take pictures from the same spot to try to duplicate the historical photograph's perspective to see how the site has changed. Then photograph the picture from the book and include it among your slides (most old photographs are in the public domain and are reprinted out of courtesy, not copyright. Besides, you'll be copying the photograph for your personal enjoyment, not for publication).
- New Mexico has something in abundance for photographers surpassing other states: dramatic, cloud-filled skies. Emphasize those skies in your photographs. Remember, however, that you may need to compensate for bright skies by changing the camera's aperture. Consult your manual for suggestions. See the photographs at Cabezon (page 32), La Liendre (page 25), and Lake Valley (page 112) for examples of photographs improved immensely by their skies.
- Although dawn and dusk generally offer the most dramatic photographic possibilities,

those times are not the most practical for people taking full-day tours. The fact is, good photographs can be taken with a quality camera under almost any conditions. Some of my favorite photographs of ghost towns were taken on dismal, gloomy days; those pictures convey a desolation and abandonment that sunshine would only have abated. See Tiptonville (page 20) and La Cueva (page 21) for examples of "dull day" photographs.

APPENDIX E: DRIVING AND WALKING IN NEW MEXICO

Survival tips are far too important to be relegated to an appendix of a ghost town book. Your local civil defense agency should have a pamphlet on the subject, and several good books have been written for the hiker and for the four-wheel drive owner.

The following guidelines are **not** intended to replace definitive books on survival techniques.

General Suggestions

1. Let someone know exactly where you're going. Show them on a map.
2. Have a good map with you.
3. Have a compass and know how to use it.
4. Have plenty of water with you, at least one gallon per person per day.
5. Carry ice in a cooler in case of snake or insect bites.
6. Have the necessary tools (see "Your Car," right).
7. Have the necessary survival gear (see "Survival Kit," right).
8. If your car breaks down and you are many miles from help, you are probably best off staying with the vehicle—especially in the desert heat. Use your signaling devices when appropriate (see "Survival Kit," right).
9. If you plan to do a good deal of backroads driving, you should consider installing a citizens' band (CB) radio in your car or truck. CB radios are reasonably priced and can summon aid quickly in case of emergency.
10. Above all, STAY CALM. Don't do anything until you have logically evaluated an emergency situation.

You

Know your limitations. The desert or mountainside is no place to determine if you are in good physical shape. If you require some sort of medication, be certain that there is an adequate supply in the survival kit. Wear comfortable clothing, including a hat, and shoes designed for walking; boots are best. Carry a watch (and a compass, canteen, and knife if you're walking any distance from the car). Know the temperature extremes in the area during a given time of year and have clothes in the car in anticipation of those extremes.

Your Car

Make sure your car is in excellent mechanical condition before you go anywhere on the back roads. Especially check tires, radiator hoses, belts, and all fluid levels. Check that the spare tire is inflated properly. Carry a set of tools, spare belts, a good jack, at least one quart of oil, fuses, jumper cables, fire extinguisher, electrical tape, duct tape, baling wire or an equivalent, flares, a shovel, a gas siphon, and perhaps a can of Fix-a-Flat for temporary tire repairs. If yours is a four-wheel drive vehicle and you're going deep into the back country, you need to carry a lot more. Consult your manual or a book on the subject.

Survival Kit

The following, adapted from a kit recommended in a Civil Defense brochure "Your Plan for Survival," should be in your car at all times:

1. Small first aid kit
2. Swiss Army knife
3. Waterproof matches
4. Good compass with a protected face
5. "Thunderer" whistle
6. Signaling mirror
7. Magnifying glass—for starting fires
8. Large-eyed needles and linen thread
9. Parachute silk, bright orange—for shelter, protecting the face in sandstorms, straining water, and signaling
10. Aluminum foil

11. Water purification tablets
12. Large orange balloons—for water storage or signaling
13. Candles
14. Razor blade
15. Pencil and note paper—for leaving notes or marking a trail
16. Adhesive tape
17. Fish hooks—for setting snares
18. Assorted nails
19. Snakebite kit (although ice and a drive to a hospital is probably preferable)
20. A sharp belt knife
21. Parachute-type tow rope
22. Blankets

All of the above items, except for the last two, fit compactly into a container about the size of an overnight bag.

Remember: have plenty of water. All of those cold cans of soft drinks will not be what you'll want or need if you get stranded.

APPENDIX F: BICYCLING TO NEW MEXICO GHOST TOWNS

New Mexico is a natural place to tour by bicycle, particularly in the Santa Fe, Taos, Las Vegas, and Raton areas in the warmer months. Many ghost towns in this volume stand along good paved roads, although some roads are rather narrow and many cross hilly or even mountainous terrain. Ghost town adventurers accustomed to touring by bicycle might consider:

Chapter One: The Madrid-Cerrillos-Golden area.

Chapter Two: Watrous to Fort Union and Watrous to La Cueva.

Chapter Four: Taos to Raton (see Trip 1, p. 58), for serious riders only; Raton to Sugarite, Yankee, and perhaps—for the more adventurous—even to Bell and Folsom.

Chapter Five: Santa Rosa to Puerto de Luna.

Chapter Six: Carrizozo to Lincoln; Carrizozo to White Oaks and Ancho.

Chapter Eight: Cuchillo to Winston (uphill but beautiful); Hillsboro to Kingston; Hillsboro to Lake Valley.

Chapter Nine: Silver City to Pinos Altos; Silver City to Hanover and Fierro.

Chapter Ten: Lordsburg to Valedon (occasionally rough road); Deming to Columbus (often windy).

Chapter Twelve: Glenwood to Graham; Glenwood to Mogollon (spectacular, but narrow and mountainous route—for the serious rider only).

BIBLIOGRAPHY

Principal sources for this book are:

Jenkinson, Michael, with Kernberger, Karl. *Ghost Towns of New Mexico: Playthings of the Wind.* Albuquerque: University of New Mexico Press, 1967.

Looney, Ralph. *Haunted Highways: The Ghost Towns of New Mexico.* Albuquerque: University of New Mexico Press, 1968.

Meleski, Patricia F., with Meleski, R. P. *Echoes of the Past: New Mexico's Ghost Towns.* Albuquerque: University of New Mexico Press, 1972.

Pearce, T. M., ed. *New Mexico Place Names: A Geographical Dictionary.* Albuquerque: University of New Mexico Press, 1965.

Sherman, James E. and Barbara H. *Ghost Towns and Mining Camps of New Mexico.* Norman: University of Oklahoma Press, 1975.

Other sources consulted include:

Beck, Warren A., and Haase, Ynez D. *Historical Atlas of New Mexico.* Norman: University of Oklahoma Press, 1969.

Brown, Dee. *Bury My Heart at Wounded Knee.* New York: Holt Rinehart and Winston, 1971.

Carter, William. *Ghost Towns of the West.* Menlo Park, California: Lane Publishing Co., 1978.

Crosby, Harry H. "The Great Diamond Fraud," in *The American Heritage Book of Great Adventures of the Old West.* New York: American Heritage Press, 1969.

El Paso Times, 18 February 1968.

Florin, Lambert. *New Mexico, Texas Ghost Towns.* Seattle: Superior Publishing Co., 1971.

Frontier Times, Feb.–March 1980.

Giese, Dale F. *Echoes of the Bugle.* Phelps Dodge booklet, n.d.

Hill, Rita. *Then and Now, Here and Around Shakespeare.* Lordsburg, N.M.: private printing, 1963.

Jenkins, Myra Ellen, and Schroeder, Albert H. *A Brief History of New Mexico.* Albuquerque: University of New Mexico Press, 1974.

Johnson, Robert Neil. *Southwestern Ghost Town Atlas.* Susanville, California: Cy Johnson and Son, 1968.

King, Scottie. *Listen to the Wind.* Published by *New Mexico Magazine,* 1978.

Los Angeles Times, 21 May 1967.

New Mexico Magazine, July 1978, September 1978, January 1979, March 1979, April 1980.

New York Times, 28 March 1903.

Parker, Morris, (edited with Introduction by C. L. Sonnichsen) *White Oaks: Life in a New Mexico Gold Camp 1880–1900.* Tucson: University of Arizona Press, 1971.

The Rustler (Cerrillos, N.M.) 8 March 1979, 11 June 1979, 19 November 1979.

Schmidt, Raymond. *New Mexico Recollections.* Private printing, 1977.

Southern Living, September 1979.

Stanley, F. *The Loma Parda Story.* Nazareth, Texas: Private printing, 1969.

Weis, Norman. *Helldorados, Ghosts and Camps of the Old Southwest.* Caldwell, Idaho: Caxton Printers, 1977.

Woods, Betty. *Ghost Towns and How to Get to Them.* Santa Fe: Sunstone Press, 1978.

MAPS

Quadrangle Maps of the State of New Mexico, New Mexico State Highway Department.

United States Geological Survey: topographic maps of New Mexico, Arizona, and Colorado.

MISCELLANEOUS BROCHURES

From: Ancho—My House of Old Things
Fort Union
Las Vegas—"Twelve Tours" and "Historic Las Vegas"
Silver City—"This is Silver City"

INDEX

Page numbers in italics indicate photographs.